Other Books by John I

A Guide to Help You Decide – Is A Travel Trailer the Right Choice for Me?

Your Guide to Purchasing a Travel Trailer

A Guide to Enjoying Your Travel Trailer

I Go Where I'm Towed – Travel Trailer Stories spanning 35 years

Remember Your Stay – A Campers Log Book

Growing Older on Two Wheels – From Tricycle to RAGBRAI

Simple Home Brewing – Brewing Ale Step by Step

A 1966 Beetle Obsession

John M Patterson

Table of Contents

Foreword

It is my pleasure to write this brief forward to John's book. We began our friendship and love of old Volkswagens in the mid-1970s in Madison, Wisconsin. Outside of a vintage British sports car perhaps, there was no better vehicle to tool around a college town than an old VW Bug.

My first car was a 1972 Beetle which I bought in 1978. After driving it for a few years I began to crave an older model. I loved the old-style dashboard, steering wheel, floor shift, the smaller windows and lights; really the whole look of those cars. So, I found a 1963 model which was mechanically sound but didn't look too hot (John can vouch for my initial buyer's remorse). After sinking $1,200 into the body and trim I finally had what I wanted.

Many times, while driving that car, people would give me a thumbs up or praise the car at a stop light or filling station; once while parked at a college parking lot, I returned to the Bug to find a note offering to buy it attached to my windshield. Sometimes on a warm night I'd just go out and sit in the car for half an hour, looking at the dashboard, gauges and steering wheel in the moonlight. In my mind I had my very own time machine.

Even though I parted with that car 36 years ago, I still keep a pristine 1963 VW Bug owner's manual as a reminder of a magical time in my life.

Dennis Trumble
Cohoes, NY

Wow, thanks for your kind words. Your beetle looks brand new! And – it's next to another good-looking beetle. I get lonesome for an old beetle from time to time. Safe Roads. Eve

John Muir's wife Eve, replying to a message I sent her in 2010.

Chapter 1 – Then Quit Your Job

My Story actually begins before I even had a driver's license. My neighbor Johnny, and I had been in the planning stages of what vehicles we would buy once we had our driver's license and jobs in order to buy gas.

The plan involved owning Volkswagen beetles and traveling from Wisconsin to California. The VW Beetle had been chosen, by us, as the most economical way to see the country.

We painstakingly mapped our route on a huge atlas state by state. Now the easy part was complete, but what would happen next?

Well as it turned out, nothing! Our lives diverged shortly after our planning phase; as life took over. My friend moved on to further his education, at a city school; and I moved on with my education. We ended up seeing very little of each other after that. Although I would still maintain a very close relationship with his family.

The summer of my sophomore year, I became a "project" for my dad. He told me that I needed to get a job, and for some odd reason, he thought being a caddy at the nearby golf course would be a great money-making opportunity. He couldn't have been more wrong.

He dropped me off each morning for a week, and I sat in that caddy shack all day, while the elite caddies took all the business. They made certain that I wouldn't be caddying on their course.

My dad gave up on that idea after a week but told me to go out on my own and find a job. That is how I landed my first "real" job. I filled out an application at a nursing home on the east side of Madison, and began working second shift.

I can tell you from personal experience, a nursing home is no place for a 16-year-old to be working. There is entirely too much drama. In addition, the owner's wife was more than a few bricks short of a full load.

I had three events that are burned into my brain while working there. One involves being grabbed violently by a ninety-year-old woman that had the strength of ten men. The second involved watching the owners' wife eat out of a garbage pail. The third was being locked in the blast freezer. Yet, I continued working there; all of that fun for $1.90 per hour.

Soon school was starting again and that posed a problem. I had been using my mom's car to go to work. That would not be available to me anymore because she was a high school teacher and would need her own transportation. A friend had a VW Karman Ghia for sale at reasonable price. When I told my dad I needed a car for work because school was starting, he said "Quit your job!" I was left wondering what this whole "get a job" exercise had been about.

So, as a result, I wouldn't have a job the rest of my high school career, because Dad didn't want anything to do with the need for an extra vehicle. I think more than anything else, he probably didn't want to deal with another car in the driveway and paying additional insurance.

Then, after high school I began a job at the State Job Service. I rode my bike the 5 miles to work every morning, dodging car doors and pedestrians. It was for the most part an uphill ride on the way there. After I arrived at work, I would lock my 10 speed to the bike rack.

After work, I would ride full speed down East Washington Avenue from the capital square. Almost always passing cars on my way home. I would stop at a grocery store that was close to my place, and pick up dinner, and then bike the remaining two blocks home.

Of course, this kind of transportation is great when it is warm. As everyone knows though, Wisconsin never stays warm for very long. I knew it was just a matter of time before I would be facing the fall weather, and then the winter.

It was at that point that I started thinking about getting a car.

Chapter 2 – Don't you buy that car John Boy.

To talk about the employees at the job center would be like trying to describe a high functioning yet dysfunctional family.

The office was split into what was called "The Professional Unit" and the "Unprofessional Unit." The Professional Unit dealt with anyone looking for work that had a college degree. The Unprofessional Unit, dealt with everyone else.

Besides finding jobs for the unemployed, the office also helped folks fill out unemployment forms and answer a myriad of questions.

The majority of the folks that came to our office were decent hard-working folks that just needed some help finding a job. A small portion of the population were people that really needed some serious mental health help.

One individual thought he worked for the FBI, and a few of the guys in the professional unit would play along. Playing along in this case involved things like writing some random numbers on a tic tack toe pattern and then handing it to him and saying "We know that you know what to do with this." Of course, he would nod and take the paper and disappear for a few days.

On one occasion they gave him a note that said something like "The Zebra will meet you in Miami, Florida, at the airport." He disappeared again, but did call from Florida a few weeks later.

I know this sounds amusing, but it was actually a pretty horrible place to work. However, to an 18-year-old the money was really, really good.

As fall approached, one of the men that worked in the professional unit and I became pretty good friends. John, was a smart guy but a pretty big drinker and often times would come to work a little hung over.

On these occasions he would always say "John Boy" which they all called me "We need to get a greasy burrito for lunch." This was his cure all for a hangover.

It was on one of our lunch excursions that I told John that I needed to get a car before winter hit. He said "Fine John Boy, let's get a greasy burrito and then we'll go look at cars."

We headed down to Park Street to get lunch and afterwards we stopped into Park "Bug Town" Motors. The building still stands today, but the parking lot was replaced with a Midas Muffler Shop sometime after they went out of business.

Bug Town didn't deal with new cars, just used vehicles, primarily VW's. My eyes immediately caught site of a Volkswagen Beetle on the side lot. I walked over to look at it and I heard John yell "John Boy, don't you buy that car."

He came over and started telling me all the reasons that it would be a bad purchase. For one thing it was nine years old. John told me the age alone, would make it a horrible car.

Now, at the time, anything foreign had to be better than what the US car makers were producing. It was almost a miracle to get 100,000 miles on a US manufactured car. That was not the case with a lot of the foreign makes. So, I wasn't too dissuaded.

This bug came from California recently so the body was solid as a rock. It also had been painted "Sun Bug Gold" or a color very close to that.

The inside of the car, well that was a different story. It had been modernized to some extent with gas, brake, and clutch pedals that looked like bare feet. It also had been outfitted with a racing steering wheel. The 1966 model year seats had been replaced with high back bucket seats from a much newer beetle.

I knew absolutely nothing about VW Beetles, but I knew that I liked this car. So, despite John's warning, I bought the car. As it turns out, I would have been wise to heed John's warning, at least on that bug.

Now oddly, there was a huge amount of paint missing from the driver's door. It looked like someone had just peeled a semi round section of paint off. I asked the salesman what had happened to the door and he said "We did that, we had to…when it came to our lot it had a huge decal of Pluto (Disney's Pluto) mounting a Volkswagen beetle, and it said "Humping to Please" underneath it." He then gave me the name of a body shop that could match the paint, and refinish the door so it would look new again.

It was with a lot of excitement that I bought the bug, and obtained my insurance. Then I dropped it off at the body shop and a few days later I picked up my very first car, a 1966 VW Beetle Sedan.

My bug came equipped with almost nothing. It had no seat belts, which were actually an option in 1966. It did not have the pop out rear windows either. It did come with a whopping six-volt electrical system. Despite this fact, it actually did a pretty fair job lighting up the road at night.

I now had my bug, and with that came the joy of driving a manual transmission. I loved everything about the car, and like any 18 year old, I liked manually shifting the car. It made me feel like I was a more active driver.

On my first decent drive on the highway, I heard a racket to the rear of the car. I immediately pulled over and found that the tires were retreads. Retreads are a cheap alternative to decent tires. They are basically remanufactured tires, with new tread bonded to an old tire.

My first stop, after getting back on the road was to Farm and Fleet, for some brand-new tires. They were Duralon, relatively inexpensive, and actually manufactured by Firestone Tires.

These were really nice tires. The 66 bug weighed very little at 1700 pounds, so just 425 pounds would be on each tire. Due to that low weight, the tires would probably dry rot before the tread would wear out.

I hoped at this point, that this would be the last money I would need to spend for a while. However, that wouldn't be the case; not by a longshot.

Chapter 3 – Unsafe at Any Speed

I decided to take my car over to show my mom and dad after I got the new tires on it. It was, in my eyes, a wonderful vehicle. My dad felt much differently.

"Judas Priest" my dad exclaimed "Didn't you read what Ralph Nadar said about those cars...Unsafe at any speed."

Ralph Nadar is probably best known for his expose on the rear-engine Chevrolet Corvair. He referred to it as "The Sporty Corvair–The One-Car Accident."

Now, my dad had tried his best to instill a certain amount of fear in us about motorcycles. When we would take vacations and he saw motorcycles he would always talk about how "crazy" it was to own one. This Ralph Nadar reference was now an attempt to disparage the bug somehow, and probably instill some fear in me.

"That was about the Corvair" I responded.

"It doesn't matter" he shot back "It's got an engine in the back and nothing in the front.

"Mom has a Corvair" I said, pointing at the garage.

"Yeah well, she just drives that to school and back. You are going to get killed in that thing!"

"Dad, I am not going to get killed in that thing."

That's where the conversation ended. Dad walked away and Mom said "I think it's very nice."

Believe me, this was not a one-time conversation. It would be a repetitive topic at the Patterson house almost every time I would visit.

Well, there is no pleasing everyone. I just got back in the bug and drove back to my place.

"My Place" was actually a house owned by my friend Mark. I rented a room from Mark, but basically, I had run of the house. It was in an older neighborhood on Waubesa Street. The neighbors were a tight knit group that looked out for each other.

On one side of the house, we had a fire chief. On the other side, we had George and Ethel. They were a retired couple, probably in their 70's at the time.

My first morning living there, I woke up to someone shouting "You woke us up! You woke us up!" This shouting was coming from directly out my window on the first floor. I thought for sure some neighborhood brawl was about to take place.

I slowly pulled back the curtain and looked out. Then I saw George across from me inside his house screaming at his Parakeet "Dicky Bird."

I grew to love George and his wife. They were very nice people. George, I found out was a parakeet lover, and this was just one of a long string of Dicky Birds. Personally, I can't imagine naming all of my pets the same name.

Mark told me that George was loud because he was pretty deaf. Later George would get hearing aids and the mornings were much more peaceful on Waubesa street.

Across the street from us was a young family. The father's name was Jose. Jose was a great guy, and very protective of our section of Waubesa Street. He was like the neighborhood watch.

I felt relatively safe parking my bug on the street in front of the house each night.

During the day, I was now driving to the job service. No more worries about rain, or the impending winter weather.

At work, the employees had a system. The system was to thwart the city of Madison's parking enforcement. Someone would be assigned to go out and look at the tires of the cars on the side streets. If they had a chalk mark on them, then a red card was prominently displayed on a rack where all employees could see it. Then they would go out and move their cars.

If there was no chalk, a green card was displayed. Later there was an older gentleman "Roy", who would go out and rub the chalk marks off the tires. At least that's what he told me he was doing.

Now, this in reality is a simplified version of how the parking alert system worked. It was a bit more involved and included personalized cards of each vehicle in a rack that would be moved behind the green or red cards if only some vehicles were chalked. My card was a Gold VW Beetle with my high school graduation picture cut out and placed in the driver's windshield to look like I was driving.

However, I liked getting chalked. It allowed me to take a break and go move my car.

Roy really liked my beetle, and we would often walk in the same direction after work. I found him to be an interesting character that had a lot of colorful stories. He told me he really liked my beetle, and kept an eye out for it when he was doing his "parking enforcement" work.

Roy, also, for some strange reason, had an irrational fear of a three-legged dog, that lived in a house next to the job center. I never understood why, but he warned me about the dog, and would never take his eyes off of it when we would pass the house.

The weekend approached and I was eager to take the VW somewhere beyond the city of Madison. Mark suggested that we take a ride to Lodi Wisconsin. Marks hobby at the time was photography, which later became his profession. He wanted to take some pictures at Gibraltar Rock State Park.

Gibraltar was only 35 miles from our place, so I thought that would be a nice ride. Mark was pretty excited to take his first ride in my bug. That would change about thirty minutes later.

As we headed into the outskirts of Lodi, a city not far from Gibraltar Rock, I crossed a set of rail road tracks and lost total control of the steering. I fought to keep the bug on the road as it veered onto the right shoulder of the road.

Mark and I got out and looked at the car. It had a sickening lean to the right front side. "Oh no…. what's going on here?" I climbed under to look but not being very mechanically inclined at the time didn't realize the severity of the issue.

I turned to Mark and said "It looks like some joint needs to be reattached to the front axle." Mark who worked third shift, was now agitated "John Boy, I have to go to work tonight, we need to get back to Madison."

We walked into Lodi and I called for a tow truck. When the driver arrived, he looked underneath the bugs' front end and I asked "Can you just put it back together?" He just smiled and said "Nope, your front ball joints are shot, they need to be replaced."

Mark took care of the tow truck bill, and I paid him back when we got home. Fortunately, Mark did make it to work on time, but just barely.

One thing to keep in mind, is that this is 1975 and Madison just happens to be the "Bug Capital" of the U.S. or so it seemed.

There were a ton of VW repair shops. However, it was in no way like it is today where you can google reviews, prices, etc. you just had to go on "Word of Mouth" from other folks. I ended up having the bug towed to Bruns Volkswagen on Highway 51.

It didn't take long before they told me the front end needed to be overhauled. The tow truck driver had been correct, it needed all new ball joints. It would cost two hundred and seventy dollars. That is an equivalent of fifteen hundred dollars in today's currency. I didn't have it.

I authorized the work and told the service manager; it would be a week before I could pick it up. I would need to wait for my next pay check.

The following week, I picked up the bug and Mark and I finally made it to Gibraltar Rock. Certainly, my bug repairs were now a thing of the past, and they were for a month or two.

John at the job service reminded me more than a few times that I should have listened to him about buying the bug. I would just shrug and tell him that I still liked it.

In the weeks that followed I became less and less thrilled about working at the Job Service. I was definitely the youngest one working there, and all of the employees in my unit were older females. My direct Supervisor whom we shall call "E", was not easy to work for. Even some of the other employees in different units expressed their sympathy for my situation.

Around this time, I began having conversations with a neighbor, John Senior, that lived across the street from my parents. He was a second father to me. He owned his own company that was a medical supply house. He needed a shipping and receiving clerk and wondered if I was interested.

I said yes immediately. As I was growing up, I had spent most of my time at John and his wife Anne's house hanging out with their kids which were all close to my age. They treated me as if I were one of their own, I even vacationed with them in the summer. To say I was excited about working for John Senior, would be an understatement.

In addition, now I would get to drive 33 miles one way to work each day on a pretty decent county road. This was going to be great.

Chapter 4 – I'll push you, John Boy.

The fall of 1975 was upon us. My friend "Boomer" had just bought his first brand new car, a beige 1975 AMC Gremlin. I loved the look of it and secretly wondered when I would ever be able to buy a new car.

Boomer and my other buddy Dennis were always coming over to Marks house and we spent a lot of time hanging out together. The three of us had known each other since I was 15 or 16, so we had been hanging out for years. When we were together, it was a laugh fest. Almost always my gut would be sore from all the laughing that would take place.

About this time, I started referring to my bug as the "little brown bear" because it looked that way at night as it sat on the street dimly lit by the porch light. Both Boomer and Dennis had an appreciation for the beetle as basic transportation. However, during the winter months, if we were going somewhere together, it probably wasn't going to be in the beetle. It was just easier to climb into Boomers car, and of course it was quite a bit roomier than the bug.

As the fall weather set in, the drive to work each morning was great. I would stop for gas, some candy, and a large bottle of coke, and then leave for work. The cooler weather allowed me to use the heat for a change. Now with the windows closed, it became a much quieter ride to work.

Wisconsin is a beautiful state. Highway 12/18 leading to Fort Atkinson from Madison was no exception. The farmland, tobacco fields, and the old farmhouses along the way were beautiful. I absolutely loved the drive.

It was twenty miles from Madison to the town of Cambridge. A beautiful old town where John Senior had once suggested that I find an apartment to rent. This would have been convenient for John because Fort Atkinson was only ten miles up the road from Cambridge. However, I had no interest in renting a place in that town because all of my friends lived in Madison.

If the fall drive was beautiful, it was even more so when winter began to set in. The snow would blanket everything in a white powder. No matter how deep the snow would get, it could never stop the beetle from making its way to Fort Atkinson.

The bottom of a classic beetle is like a toboggan. The floor pans make up the majority of the underside of the car. There's a tunnel that divides the floor pans, but it really doesn't stick down very far at all. As a result, you basically sled down the road with the engine weight directly over the rear tires providing traction. I would be driving the beetle in the snow when others probably wouldn't even attempt it.

It wasn't long after the first snowfall of 1975 that I started having issues with my starter. I would turn the key, and nothing would happen. Fortunately for me, Waubesa street was relatively flat and the car was relatively light. So, I would push the car down the road as fast as I could, then jump in and pop the clutch to start it.

This worked pretty good for the first month or so, because quite frankly I was broke. While I loved working in Fort Atkinson, the pay was substantially less than what I had made at the state job service. A new starter was just not in the budget at this point.

Then one day, we got a pretty decent snowfall and I couldn't push the car. The street was covered in a compacted snow that had been created by cars grinding the snow down into a consistency very close to that of ice. Without any traction for my tennis shoes, I was unable to push the beetle. Mark who had just got home from his third shift job at the bakery said "Don't worry John Boy, I'll give you a push with the wagon." Although I felt uncomfortable with doing this, it seemed like the only way I was going to get to work that day.

Mark lined up his old station wagon with the rear bumper of my bug and began pushing it. As soon as I popped the clutch, his front bumper slid over mine. This resulted in a huge dent when his bumper impacted the engine lid of my beetle.

I got out of the bug while it was idling to look at the damage. "Sorry John Boy, I didn't think that would happen." I lifted the engine lid and pushed on the dent, and miraculously, it popped out perfectly. There was no indication it had ever been dented. I took off for work just happy that the car was running and that I didn't have a dent.

That event spelled the end of my mornings pushing the bug down Waubesa Street. I needed to get a starter and find a new VW shop where I could get mechanical work done.

A day or two later, I looked through the yellow pages of the phone book and found "Tom's Barn." Tom's Barn was a VW repair shop on an old farm property on Raymond Road in Madison. I guess you know you've made the big time when you don't need to list your address on your advertisement. The yellow page advertisement said "Next to the channel 3 tower on Raymond Road"

Guess what? It wasn't hard to find either! I just looked for the tower, then I saw the barn and a multitude of VW's.

As I pulled up to the driveway that led to the "Barn", there was a sign for his shop that was taken from John Muir's book on VW repair. The drawing, created by Peter Aschwanden, showed three men lifting a beetle's rear bumper into the air while the bugs engine lay on the ground.

*Illustration by Peter Aschwanden. Reprinted with permission from the Aschwanden family.

A few minutes later I met Tom inside the barn. The smell of parts cleaner, oil, and gas hung in the air. There was something very appealing about this place to an 18-year-old. All the tools, beetles, grease, and just the thought of being able to fix beetles for a living, it was cool. The only thing that was missing was a decent forced air furnace. It was cold in the barn.

Tom was a thirty something, shaggy haired guy that just happened to be an expert mechanic, and reasonable in his prices. I don't think there was anything that Tom couldn't fix.

Tom replaced the starter for a great price and I enjoyed talking with him. Looking at all the beetles that were in the process of being repaired, I felt very fortunate that Tom had worked my repair into his schedule. This was obviously a very popular VW repair shop.

In retrospect, I should have asked Tom about the maintenance that is required for a 1966 VW Beetle. Not knowing about air cooled engines would certainly end up being a mistake on my part.

By now I was getting a lot of things fixed on the bug. I had probably invested well over five hundred dollars in repairs so far. Even so, I still had not regretted purchasing the bug despite all of that.

Winter of 1975 was now in full swing. If you know classic beetles, you understand the heating system in the 66 provides very little to absolutely no heat to the front windshield in a Wisconsin winter. If it's just cold weather, well that's one thing, but if it's a heavy snow storm with icing, that's something completely different.

Keep in mind, there's no way to correct for that problem, unless you wanted to install a gas heater. That's right, VW offered a heater that used gasoline to provide extreme heat that had no control other than having it "on" or "off." Even though I had heard other bug owners talk about how safe they were, I had absolutely no interest in something that sounded that dangerous.

My solution was to scrape the frost off the inside of the windshield with an ice scraper. When the snow and ice would pile up on the outside, I would roll down my window and repeat that process on the outside of the windshield directly in front of me.

I didn't feel uncomfortable doing this occasionally, but it was a bit of a hassle.

It became a much larger hassle when the wiper motor quit a few weeks into some pretty nasty winter weather. Then it was a quick trip to Toms, and he installed a new wiper motor in the bug while I watched. I would still need to scrape the windshield occasionally but at least the wipers were working again.

I still had a lot of winter to deal with, and things were about to get worse…much worse.

Chapter 5 – Merry Christmas.

It was now the week before Christmas. I had been working in Fort Atkinson for about three months at this point.

It was a bitterly cold morning, pitch black with a few snow flurries. I was going over a long bridge on highway 51 towards highway 12. Suddenly I heard a loud racket. It sounded like I was dragging a couple of garbage cans behind me.

Then my two dash lights (Oil and Generator) came on, as if I had turned the car off. Now the horrible sound behind the car stopped and it was replaced with complete silence. I pulled the car onto the shoulder of the highway and got out to look at the engine.

There was oil everywhere under my bug. I didn't know exactly what had happened at that point, but I knew it wasn't good at all, and that it was going to result in a new motor being required. "Merry Christmas" I said sarcastically as I walked across the highway on my mile long walk to a PDQ store.

This moment would later be reflected in a Birthday Card given to me in March of 1976 by Dennis. On the front cover of the card it shows Charlie Brown saying he has a special Birthday Message for me. Next to that Dennis had written "But you don't want to hear that message." On the inside cover is his depiction of me that early December morning; three months earlier, walking away from a blown engine with the Capital of Madison in the background. A pretty good depiction. I could laugh about it then, but not in the moment.

But back to my misery: I was not really dressed appropriately for a break-down. Boomer and I had bought some army surplus trench coats, earlier in the year. We thought they looked cool, and that was basically my winter attire that day. Needless to say, that did not provide the kind of warmth I needed on my hike.

From the PDQ I made two phone calls. One call to my employer who found a ride for me to work. The second call was for a tow truck to drop off the little bear at Tom's Barn. I felt sick to my stomach.

An hour later, Bruce who worked at the same place, picked me up at the PDQ. He was a strange guy. He spent most of the trip bitching that I had an unreliable car. A couple weeks later Bruce left for lunch and never came back to work again. According to John Senior he had taken a few payroll checks with him.

About noon, I called Toms Barn and talked to Tom. He gave me the news I dreaded. The engine needed to be rebuilt. In retrospect, I'm not sure he rebuilt that engine, since it had thrown a rod and probably had damaged the case. He probably rebuilt a different engine and put it in the car. Tom had a multitude of engines sitting on his barn's shelves.

He told me it would take about a week to get the engine back in the car. That was fine with me, I could finagle rides to work and eventually make a trip to the bank to refinance the car so I could get money to pay for the new engine.

Christmas came and went without a vehicle. I did get a chance to get to the bank and refinance the loan, borrowing my dad's Buick LeSabre. So now it seemed like everything would fall into place. I would just need a ride out to Tom's Barn to pick up the bug.

That ride came from a most unexpected source, my dad. The anti VW Guy himself.

We pulled into the driveway leading to Toms Barn, and I could see my bug up ahead off to the left of the barn. I was already pretty excited to be getting it back.

My dad then asked if I wanted him to stay and I said "No, it's ready to go, this won't take long." So, Dad went his way, I went inside to talk to Tom.

The 1975 Tom's Barn Yellow Pages Ad: You know you're popular with an address that ambiguous. Obviously, Peter Aschwandens' illustration was used without permission in this advertisement.

Tom talked me through the specifics of what he required from me during the engine break-in period, and then told me that he wanted to change the oil after two weeks. Then he made a suggestion that changed the way I lived with my bug. He said "John, get a copy of John Muir's book on VW repair. You need to learn how to do valve adjustments. You can do that, it's easy…or you can bring it back here every three thousand miles and I will do it. It will be cheaper if you do it, but you decide. It needs to be done!"

I bought the book the next day and read it almost cover to cover over the next month. John Muir was actually a big fan of the 1966 model and he stated *"The '66 Beetle is my personal favorite. The 1300 engine was powerful, frugal on gas, and could wail at high RPM all day if asked. This is an excellent collectable that can double as a daily driver, strong and well-constructed."*

In addition to John Muir, the guru of VW repair approving my choice of the '66, his book had wonderful illustrations by Peter Aschwanden that made repair and maintenance a pretty easy job. After Tom did the additional valve adjustments and oil changes that were required when the engine was in the break-in period, I began doing my own.

I would lay on my back in the road in front of the house on Waubesa Street and change the oil, then the next morning I would adjust the valves with a cold engine.

Tom was right, doing valve adjustments was not complicated. I learned the hard way what John Muir stated in his book ""Come to kindly terms with your ass, for it bears you!" In other words, give the beetle what it needs to survive, because if you don't, you will be without transportation.

I had always loved the smell of the beetle. Not just the way the interior smelled, but also the way it smelled when it was running.

Anyone that has ever owned a classic beetle knows exactly what I'm talking about in regards to the interior smell. Some people say that the smell is a result of the horse hair seat padding. Others say it is a smell given off by the materials that make up the headliner, seat covers, and the door panels. I have no idea what caused the smell, but I loved it. I would have friends climb in the car and say "Ahhh..the VW smell."

The beetle also had a unique smell when it ran. Now with my rebuilt engine, the smell was slightly different. It seemed like it was comprised of exhaust and parts cleaner. It smelled what I imagined a new air-cooled engine would smell like.

I was really enjoying my 1966 bug now. It ran flawlessly, and I was relieved knowing that there wasn't much more that could possibly go wrong mechanically. The transmission was solid, the engine, front end, wiper motor, and starter were brand new.

Realistically, the car was almost completely rebuilt. There were things that I wanted to change though. I wanted to change its strange California influence back to more of a stock 1966 look. That was going to take money, so that would need to wait.

In particular, I really wanted to change the chrome bumpers. The California owners had replaced those with a one-piece chrome rail in the front and back. I didn't like the looks of it. It was obvious that they were trying to modernize a 1966, and that just didn't work, at least not for me.

The dash had been painted the same color as the exterior but it had streaks where the paint had been applied too thick and resulted in the downward movement of the paint before it could set. It looked pretty horrible. I fixed that by putting a woodgrain veneer over it, which was inexpensive and looked better than the paint.

Then there were just little odds and ends things, that wouldn't cost much money and were readily available at J.C. Whitney. Even today J.C. Whitney is still in business and carrying some parts for the 66 beetle, although not nearly as much today. They were a low-cost alternative for an 18-year-old kid on a limited budget.

I eventually purchased door seals, wiper arms, a dome light, and other small parts. Since the car was mechanically sound, I could now concentrate on the little things.

One day in early 1976, my bug wouldn't start when I was leaving work. I knew it wasn't the battery, because that was new. I figured it had to be the ignition switch.

I opened the front hood and removed the cardboard cover that protected the wires, fuses, and dash components. I then took the wires off the ignition switch and touched them together and the starter engaged and the car started.

Since there was an auto parts store a block away, I removed the switch and walked down to the store. I wasn't sure whether a NAPA would have anything that would work in a beetle, but they had an exact replacement.

I returned to work and installed the new switch and was on my way again.

Around this time John Senior had hired some office help from the local high school intern program. I was immediately smitten by a long-haired blonde in the group, Tammy.

I will never forget the first time I saw her, standing with three other girls that were there to talk about the intern program. I was immediately attracted to her.

I took every attempt to flirt with her when she came back to run the postage meter each afternoon. I couldn't tell whether she liked me, although she did ask me what my real name was because everyone at work called me by my nickname Ratter. I told her Patterson, John Patterson, I'm nineteen and available".

As a result, I started an investigation utilizing the women in the office. Beth, who seemed to

51

know a lot about folks in town told me she was pretty sure Tammy did not have a boyfriend. So, there was hope.

I kept up my flirting with a feeling that it might actually lead to a date at some point.

Chapter 6 – Road Trip.

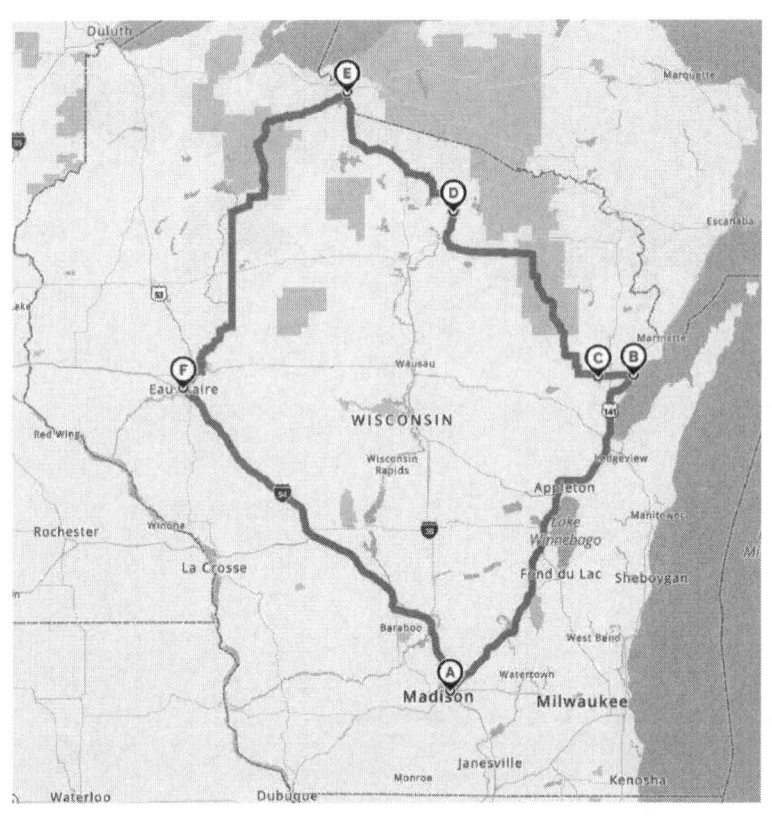

It is now late spring of 1976 and Dennis, Boomer, and I are in a band together so we saw each other all the time. We were all rather inseparable. It was pretty much like the three musketeers, or four musketeers if Mark was around.

Dennis and I probably spent the most time together, and we still stay connected today. However, Dennis now lives in New York, and I live in Texas; so it's been quite a while since we have seen each other in person, but we still talk on the phone. Back in 1976 though, we were together all the time. Dennis only lived a few blocks from Mark's place on Waubesa Street, so it was easy to get together.

One Saturday I went down to see if Dennis wanted to go for a drive out in the country. He told me that the couple he lived with were gone for the weekend and that he had agreed to take care of Bonnie, their dog. So, I figured the road trip was a no-go, but Dennis said "Let me get her out to the bathroom and we can go for a ride."

What happened next was one of the most memorable road trips although probably the most irresponsible, as Bonnie ended up being abandoned. Even today Dennis talks about how much he regrets having done that to Bonnie. I feel the same way, but as I tell Dennis "We were stupid kids."

We both hopped in the bug and took off for the gas station. I filled up my whopping ten-gallon tank and we began cruising north on highway 151.

About an hour into the drive we came to the city of Waupun, and I mentioned to Dennis that we were only another 90 minutes from Oconto. Oconto, Wisconsin happened to be where my parents were staying for the weekend. My mom grew up in Oconto, and my dad had grown up in neighboring Oconto Falls.

My understanding was that they were staying at my grandma's house in Oconto. So, I thought, well this might be a nice ride and we could surprise my folks.

Dennis, liked the idea and then said, "but remember, there's Bonnie back at the house.' We both thought this delay would be ok, and I took the turn on Highway 26.

The bug was running great, the weather was great. and we were having a blast.

Thirty minutes later, we were on highway 41 heading north to Oconto. Highway 41 is a major highway. Even though it is a highway, the scenery is still beautiful. Oshkosh, Neenah/Menasha, Appleton, and all the way north to Oconto is a beautiful drive. Back then, you could also smell the paper mills that were in the area, like Kimberly-Clark and James River. A hard to describe sweet/sour smell permeated that air from their plants.

Making things a little more entertaining along the way was a pair of girls we ran into while gassing the beetle in Oshkosh. They were definitely flirting with us, and us back with them. What ensued was a game of cat and mouse on the highway all the way to our turn off to Oconto. It was a little disappointing when they went straight, as Dennis and I had already thought about the possibility of meeting up with them again.

Now, it was on to Oconto, a short 12 miles up the road. I knew Oconto well, because we spent at least a week here every summer when we were growing up. For a kid, Oconto was terribly boring. It was a small town, that had very little to offer kids.

For my folks it was great, because we were left at grandma's house while Mom and Dad were partying with my Uncle Jack and Aunt Evie in Oconto falls, about 15 miles away.

Now, maybe that sounds like a good time was had by all. Not so much. So let me briefly tell you what life in Oconto was like for me.

Grandma and my Aunt Mable lived together, they were sisters and both widows. The house (owned by Grandma) was replete with catholic religious pictures, almost all rather graphic, and on every wall in the house. The notable exceptions were a windmill picture in the living room, that had been painted by another aunt of mine; and a large picture in the dining room of some angels playing musical instruments. For a small child, it was probably the least terrifying of the religious pictures, yet still a reminder that those angels ended up in heaven somehow.

Ruby, my grandma was born in 1885, so in the 1960's she was already in her seventies, as was Aunt Mable. When our parents left, the routine was the same...Grandma and Mable would try to keep us as quiet as possible. This almost always started with sitting on the front porch with a game they liked to call "Guess the color of the next car to drive by." Once you made your prediction, no one could talk until the next car drove by, which was infrequent.

After that it was inside to recite the rosary. This was followed by dinner, and then bingo. This was the exact same process every night. It was a routine that would have been great for a dog, because dogs absolutely love routine, but not for kids with a lot of pent up energy.

Now my sister Mary, I think she loved this, but I know I did not. Of course, Mary got to sleep in the downstairs bedroom, whereas my brother Bill and I were relegated to the creepy second story of the house for bed. We didn't even go up there during the day.

When my mom was very young, this house didn't even have a foundation. It sat on logs waiting for the foundation to be poured. She told me that in the wind you could feel the house rock back and forth on the logs.

This house had very, very limited electricity. There was some in the kitchen, and there was a power cord coming down from the ceiling leading to the TV in the living room, which for some reason we didn't get to watch very often.

There was a porch off the back side of the house that was maybe twenty or thirty feet from a set of rail road tracks. A door at the back of the kitchen led to this rickety old porch. It had been built by my great grandfather who, my dad said, "never used a tape measure during its construction." That was a fact that was apparent by just looking at it.

Each night Aunt Mable would lead Bill and I up the long narrow and steep stairway to the second floor. Due to the lack of lighting, this was done with Mable's flashlight.

Aunt Mable's flashlight would illuminate more horrifying pictures as we climbed the steps. The handrail consisted of an old galvanized water pipe that someone had bolted to the wall. Then at the very top of the stairs was my room. "Johnny, there's your bed, get in!" then she and Bill would walk through my room in order to get to his adjoining room. "Billy, there's your bed, get in!"

Now as if this isn't terrifying enough, Mabel would then hold the flashlight so we can see her face and she would say "and don't go into

Grandpa's closet!" Grandpa died the year I was born. I had no idea where his closet even was, but I sure as hell wasn't going to go look for it.

I'd lay in my bed listening for any sound of Grandpa emerging from his closet. He had to be in there, right? I mean why else would we be told "not to go in" there? Mable, not having any children of her own, probably had no idea what kind of terror any of her actions caused. This whole ordeal resulted in multiple nightmares about stumbling into Grandpa's closet, where I would happen to discover his casket.

I was always surprised, and relieved, when I would wake up the next day and still be alive.

It was now 1976, and the horrors of the past, while not forgotten, were certainly not a reason to stay away from the house on Main Street.

At this point my grandma was 91 years old, and living in a nursing home in downtown Oconto. Mable still lived in the house, but would eventually move to the nursing home just to be close to her sister. Despite Mable's actions when we were children, I realized as I grew up that she really was a warm-hearted person.

Dennis and I pulled up to the house on Main Street. There really wasn't a driveway so we just parked on the street and then knocked on the door. A very surprised Mable opened the door and shot us a big smile and said "Oh my! What are you boys doing here?" I then explained that Dennis and I were just on a Saturday ride that had turned into something more, and thought we would surprise Mom and Dad. "Well, they're not here, they're over at Jack and Evie's place in the Falls (Oconto Falls). Of course, they were…where else would they be?

Then Mabel offered us a place to stay for the night but I told her that we had to be back in Madison to take care of Bonnie, but thanked her. I gave Mable a hug, and then Dennis and I left for Oconto Falls.

The road on the way to Oconto Falls is a decent road, Highway 22. As a kid we took this road often to visit Uncle Jack. It goes through an intersection called Stiles Junction. At that intersection, there was always a Bull in a large fenced in area. I don't remember if the bull was still there when Dennis and I drove by.

Further down the road from Stile's junction was a bridge where a horrible car accident had taken place when we were kids. The first year or two after the accident, the skid marks were a remnant of the carnage that had taken place there.

Uncle Jack and Aunt Evie's house was located in the country north of the city. They had a nice ranch house on a big spread of property. It was at my Uncle Jack's where I got my first driving lesson from Dad, having just received my learners permit before our visit.

When I was younger, I loved going here for a couple of reasons. One, the atmosphere was less boring with much more to do than in Oconto. Two, and most importantly, they had a German shepherd named Tammy. I loved that dog.

I told my Uncle Jack at his 90th birthday party, a few years ago, how much I loved his dog Tammy, and it took me a long time to find a wife that had the same name. He smiled and said "Yes, she was a good girl." I'm certain that my love of German shepherds is rooted in the contact I had with his dog, as a child.

Dennis and I were now rolling up to my uncle's house. We knocked on the door but apparently the two Patterson couples were nowhere to be found. Of course, had my dad come to the door I would have gotten the "unsafe at any speed speech" again.

I was disappointed that I didn't get to see Jack. He was such a great guy. Even as kids, he would always shake our hands, and treat us as if we were adults. His demeanor was always very pleasant and friendly. My dad on the other hand, was a very serious guy, but I never saw anyone who could get my dad laughing like Jack could.

Now that we had come up empty handed, I had a thought. "Hey Denny, do you want to see Sugar Camp Lake? This was a lake where I had spent summer vacations with John Seniors family. Dennis at this point, had given up on getting back to take care of Bonnie and said "Sure, then we can cruise over to see my Uncle Orville in Eau Claire.

That sounded good to me, so off we went humming away in my 1966 beetle. The next leg of the journey would be 115 miles but take about two and a half hours.

Surprisingly the ride went very quickly and we ended up getting at Sugar Camp Lake just before sunset. This place held such great memories for me. Now, I looked out on the lake with Dennis and told him what it was like to water ski there, and how the island in the middle was covered in fire ants. Even so, we would visit the island often in the little Chrysler 9.2 Horse Powered boat; or as we always called it simply "the 9.2."

I learned a lot here in the summer. John Senior would always tell me "Push yourself, learn your limitations" and while this was related to water skiing, he also used it as a lesson about life. A lesson I never forgot.

Now a new plan emerged. "Let's drive up to Hurley Wisconsin it's by Ironwood Michigan." Dennis suggested. "Ever been there?" "Nope" was my reply.

Dennis suggested, "We can put our money together and find a motel up there for the night, get up really early and drive to Eau Claire. Then we'll have breakfast with Uncle Orville and head back to Madison. I bet we can get back in time to let Bonnie out before the folks get back."

As I mentioned, kids are stupid. I would never leave my dog alone this long. The thought that we did was selfish and inexcusable.

So off we drove towards Hurley Wisconsin. "Hurleys beautiful" Dennis remarked as we left Sugar Camp Lake. We were once again on our way.

It would be a one-and-a-half-hour drive to the Hurley Wisconsin area from Sugar Camp Lake. Even though this was a six-volt electrical system, the bug did a fairly decent job lighting up the road. What could be better than spending that amount of time with your best friend and your bug?

Going anywhere with Dennis is fun, even today. He has a unique sense of humor that is based primarily in shock value. It was not the kind of humor that would have ever gone over with my folks...but that never stopped him. I was always a little apprehensive when he would get on a roll in front of my parents. However, my parents came to terms with his sense of humor, and seemed unaffected but probably not nearly as amused as I was. So, needless to say, our ride north was filled with a boat load of laughter, and it wasn't long and we were on the outskirts of Hurley.

Hurley has a sordid history dating back to logging times. A history that includes prostitution and gambling. We weren't going to get that lucky though, we were only staying one night.

We checked into what was probably a one- or two-star hotel and called it a night, while my little brown bear slept in their parking lot. Tomorrow would be another wonderful ride.

When we woke up the next day, we knew it was going to be a long ride to Eau Claire; 165 miles to be exact.

A cool morning and some fog greeted us as we jumped in the bug and started on our way. Soon we were clipping along past Spooner, and Rice Lake.

After the stop in Eau Claire, I knew we were still facing another three hours on the road to get back to Bonnie.

I enjoyed meeting Dennis's relatives. They were down to earth and very welcoming. We had a great breakfast and were back on our way again. Dennis looked over at me and he said "Hey John Boy...I bet Bonnie is looking out the front window right now and she's thinking "They'll be back any minute." I had a feeling she had probably been thinking that for about twelve hours.

Now, the time clicked by and soon we were pulling up in front of where Dennis lived. He made a dash inside as I walked up to the porch. Suddenly he came outside and said "Oh My God, I don't believe it, she didn't have any accidents." And I said "Well where is she now?" and Dennis responded "She's in the back yard."

I stepped in the house and then Dennis let Bonnie back inside. In a moment of extreme contempt for our long trip she decides to go to the bathroom in front of us as if to say "Take that boneheads." It was poetic justice.

Dennis had the mess cleaned up in a nick of time, just before the owners came in the door. We went down the street to the porch swing at Marks, and swore we would never tell the owners what had happened.

It had been a great trip despite our stupidity. We had travel over 700 miles in less than 24 hours. The bug performed flawlessly. I loved this beetle.

Chapter 7 – Why did you let me do that!

Summer was in the air, or close to it. I decided to go to my folks' house and see how my sister was doing. I asked her if she wanted to take a ride in the bug, and of course the answer was "Yes."

We took the same route that my mom used to make me drive when I had my learners permit. The road wound past lake Mendota, then up through Maple Bluff.

Sometime during this ride, I thought it might be cool to teach Mary how to drive the beetle. We pulled over in a big parking lot by the lake, and I went through the mechanics of how the clutch worked and how to use it.

Mary took the wheel and actually did quite well. So well in fact that I thought it would be fun to have her drive the bug back to my parents' house which was less than a half mile away.

What happened next was one of those slow-motion series of events. Mary began entering the driveway where my dad and brother Bill were standing, except she confused the clutch for the brake and we roared towards them.

They both scattered like cockroaches running in different directions while I grabbed the emergency brake, and engaged the rear brakes. The bug immediately stalled with a final lurch forward. I watched helplessly as the light post outside our front door toppled over under the force of my 1700-pound beetle.

"Jesus Christ" Bill yelled "Are you trying to kill us!" Mary looked over at me and said "Gee...why did you let me do that?"

I hopped out of the car and pulled the light post back up. The dent is still in that light post some 47 years later. Mom and Dad are gone now, but the impression of my '66 beetle still remains.

I don't remember Dad taking my head off over what happened, probably because Mary was driving. I look back now at what happened, and it's funny, but it could have been much worse.

We all went inside the house and it was for the most part forgotten; except by Bill who relayed the story to my mom, step by step, second by second.

Mom and Dad on the other hand went about their business. They were getting ready for a trip to Washougal Washington to visit my dad's brother, Mike.

I had heard stories about Mike's ranch from my Uncle Jack. He talked about being woken up early in the morning by Mike who was screaming for Bull Ramos, a bull that he had named after a professional wrestler.

Jack said he could hear him screaming over and over again "Bull Ramos"; apparently in an attempt to get the bull to come to him.

That is about all I knew of Uncle Mike, other than a short meeting at Uncle Jacks house when I was very small. My brother Bill knew Mike very well as he had gone out to his ranch a number of times as a kid.

My sister and brother both still lived at home which meant that my parents' dog, Tasha, would be taken care of while the folks were gone. Other than Tasha, I highly doubt there was anything to really worry about. Except that we were going to have a big 4th of July party at my folks' house.

My parents' house was on the very edge of Warner Park. Where a huge fireworks display was held every year, and continues to this day. This was going to be an even bigger year because it was the bi-centennial.

I picked Dennis up early in the day and we headed over. We pulled the little bug up into the driveway where it would be safe. There was no way I would trust this car on the street with all the crazy 4th of July traffic.

Mom and Dad had left for Washougal days earlier. When we arrived my old next door neighbor Steve was there. Steve lived next door to us on second street. We left that house when I was nine years old, but Steve would randomly show up over the years. I was happy to see him.

I want to preface the next story by saying that I was not a drinker. I would have a couple beers now and then, or a vodka gimlet or two with Boomer on occasion. However, I had never been really intoxicated.

Steve brought a 12 pack of beer with him to the house. He turned to me when dusk was starting and said "John, let's go down to the lagoon, so we can get the best view of the fireworks. The lagoon was where the fireworks actually launched. "Yeah sure" I replied, and off we went.

Well, the fireworks were in full swing, and the beer flowed freely, too freely. I can't tell you how much I had, but when the fireworks were over, the case of beer was empty; and I was wobbly. As soon as we stood up, Steve turned to me and said "I have to take a piss!" I didn't really think anything of that, because we were not so far from the house. However, in the midst of an enormous crowd, Steve was urinating at the edge of the woods, and I of course, am doubled over laughing hysterically.

By the time we walked back to the house, I was feeling less amused. I told Dennis he was stranded for the night, I'm not sure he was amused either; but no way I was driving. What happened next was a cold shower and a series of trips to the bathroom to purge the alcohol from my system.

The next morning, I came downstairs with my first ever hang-over greeted by Dennis who said "Feed me!" with a bit of a scowl on his face. I went to the fridge and cooked us breakfast and off we went in the little bug.

Chapter 8 – He's going to bleed to death!

It is now the middle of July, 1976. My beautiful beetle is almost where I want it to be cosmetically, and I have plans on getting the bumpers replaced soon.

I have just installed my latest purchase on the beetle; two brand new horn grilles. These are located just below each headlight. They would be the very last purchase I would make for my 1966 beetle.

Work was going well and I was loving the drive to work each day in the bug, and the prospect of seeing Tammy. I had a radio in the bug, but I would also take a battery-operated tape recorder along and play music when there was nothing good on the radio. WLS out of Chicago was my favorite radio station, but once I got beyond half way home, that signal to the beetles six-volt radio, just didn't quite make the trip.

Now, the six-volt system is an interesting piece of equipment. There is a morass of wiring leading to the fuse area and switches and then to the components. That is a lot of wire for a six-volt system to handle. The faster the car goes, the brighter the lights. It's the same with the wipers and radio. However, it put out enough light for an

18-year-olds eyes, and I drove in the dark enough to feel quite comfortable with that.

On one occasion in early July, a salesman that worked at the company was having his car repaired and asked if I could give him a ride home that night. For some reason we left work after the sun went down. George was not thrilled about being in the bug to begin with. He felt more comfortable with a lot of protection on the front end.

We were well on our way down highway 12 when I saw headlights far in the distance. It looked as if they were in our lane, but it was just an illusion.

I turned to George and asked "That cars not in our lane, is it?" and George just came unglued. As a passenger, he had a different visual on the car than I did, and he could see it was not in our lane. "God Damnit, I am never riding with you again. That car is nowhere near us, what the hell is wrong with your eyes?!!!. I want out of this car!"

Of course, I found that to be really funny and just started laughing. The rest of the trip was quite uneventful. George, true to his word, never asked me for another ride again.

The next weekend Mark and I made one of our country rides in the beetle, and on the way home we saw a guy in a convertible sports car hot dogging it for his girlfriend. I pull my little beetle up next to his sport car and Mark and I yell "woo-hoo" at him, and he goes absolutely berserk.

What ensues is a crazy road rage race between a 1966 beetle and a guy who is hanging out of his sports car screaming at the top of his lungs to "Pull over!" Mark turns to me and says "That guys nuts!" Oh, he was right, this guy was not screwed on tight at all.

At this point the lunatic is right on my rear bumper, so I quickly pull in the far-left lane, hit the brakes and as he zooms by, and I take the exit ramp he just passed.

Mark turns to me and says "My God John Boy, that was some great driving right there!" It may have been a smart move, but in my head we had just been lucky.

However, my luck was about to change. A series of events were about to take place at work that would change everything.

It is July 23rd, 1976 and John Senior is putting a brand-new computer system into the front office. Everything up to this point had been done with manual record keeping. John had given us a lecture about the new system telling us that "Our business is not going to go down if the computer crashes, so don't think that we stop working if something happens."

The person from the computer company, Gene, was a very likeable guy in his late twenties. He was always asking me if I wanted to take a ride on his motorcycle. This particular day, I said yes. That ride caused me to leave later than usual from work, nothing that I was concerned about though.

It was an ungodly hot day riding home. I had all my windows open, hoping for some relief. July is typically hot and humid in Wisconsin. In late July the corn crops are quite high. The saying is "Knee high by the fourth of July." Well, the corn now was much higher.

Cambridge, the small town between Fort Atkinson and Madison, is really the last time that I needed to come to a complete stop before Madison. It's clear sailing from Cambridge to Madison.

Even though Cambridge is a small town, they had their own traffic enforced by a sheriff named Gordon.

Gordon took radar just about every day at the bottom of the hill coming through Cambridge. He wrote me a ticket one day, and I probably was going just a little too fast, but not what I believed to be ticket worthy. Gordon was nice enough, and we actually had a good conversation about the beetle.

That particular day, coming through Cambridge later than usual, I did not see Gordon. Perhaps I just didn't notice him. I made it a habit to be in second gear going down the hill so as not to gain speed and get another ticket.

Now it was on to Madison, and hopefully relief from the heat.

About 12 miles outside of Madison is Highway W, which intersects with Highway 12/18. On that corner sat a bar called "Katie and Porky's." It was set a bit back from the intersection and the corn crop ran up almost to the edge of the intersection.

As I entered the intersection, I was probably moving at a little over 60 miles per hour. At about the point my front hood entered the intersection I saw a white flash, it was a white mustang. I thought immediately "He is going to hit me."

Apparently when the impact took place I was launched through the windshield, first by bending the steering wheel down to the left, taking off the rear-view mirror with my eye, and then launching through the glass. I ended up over the hood of the beetle, with my feet resting on the frame of the windshield. The driver who hit me had pulled me off the hood and told me later that I had been saying "I can't breathe." I have no recollection of any of that.

He moved me from the hood of the beetle out into the field next to the highway. It's rather amazing that I didn't end up getting crushed during the roll.

Both of my front seats were also launched through the windshield. Now, this wouldn't have happened had they been the correct seats for the car. Since the owner in California had put high back seats in the car, they didn't fit the floor mounting tracks. Therefore, in their wisdom, they used hose clamps to lock the seats to the floor. This was one other thing that I had hoped to change at some point.

What happened next will probably seem bizarre but I was dreaming that I was at Cops Department Store trying on sun glasses because the light was so bright. I kept trying on different pairs because they just wouldn't dull the bright light. In retrospect could it have been a near death experience? – you decide.

Then I suddenly opened my eyes and I was sitting out in my driver's seat in the middle of a tobacco patch just west of Katy and Porky's bar, on the opposite side of the road.

Katie and Porky's bar had completely emptied when they heard the crash. Now an older gentleman who looked like Colonel Sanders was looking down at me and he said "Oh…he's going to bleed to death before the ambulance gets here." I thought "Oh great, that's nice to wake up to!" Then he asked me "What happened son?" and I replied "He ran the stop sign" to which he replied "I thought so!"

His utterance was followed by someone yelling "Let's get him!" and the crowd moved towards the perpetrator of the accident. These folks obviously knew this guy, and as I would find out a few weeks later, he had a criminal record at least a mile long.

Then I heard a very familiar voice, it was Gordon's, the sheriff from Cambridge "Anyone make one more move and you are all going to jail." That settled things down for the moment.

When I looked over at the road, my beautiful bug was laying on its side. It had obviously rolled after the impact. That wasn't good. I wondered how much it would cost to get it towed to Tom's Barn for repairs.

So, my brain, obviously scrambled, could only think how pissed off my brother Bill would be when I had to call him for a ride home.

Gordon now was asking me who to call about the accident. I gave him John Seniors phone number back at work. I was sure John would get a hold of my family.

Shortly after this the ambulance arrived and the EMTs began trying to figure out what shape I was in. They later listed me in critical condition because they assumed I would have internal injuries and broken bones after such an impact. They asked me what hospital I wanted to go to, and I told them the Methodist Hospital in Madison.

Meanwhile back at work, John Senior gets the call that I've been in an accident. He doesn't think it's serious because Gordon says "He's sitting on the side of the road, in the tobacco patch." John assumes that is a good thing and relays this to Barb, Judy, and Beth, the women in the front office. At this point they are probably thinking, well this will make a good story for Monday morning.

Tammy didn't find out about the accident until the next work day. Barb, Judy, and Beth, down played the accident based on what John had told them. So, Tammy thought it was nothing serious.

At home, Bill gets a call from John Seniors wife and is told he should get to the hospital right away. Bill could see Mary at the top of the park walking towards the Lagoon, and he began to follow her. She told me later that she thought it was weird that he was following her. Once he caught up to her, he said "John's been in an accident, we're supposed to go to St. Mary's hospital."

Meanwhile, I am being rolled into the hospital emergency room and coincidentally I see a doctor that I had met a week earlier when I was visiting a friend who had a broken collar bone. I call out his name and he quickly comes over to my stretcher. I reintroduce myself, and he does a quick assessment of my injuries. He gave some brief instructions to the staff and left.

He probably would have stayed longer but he had someone coming into the ER that had jumped off the local YMCA in a botched attempt at suicide.

I was now wheeled to x-ray, then after that back to the ER for them to clean and suture my arm and back.

The ER Doctor then tells me that my arm is so mutilated that he would have to sew me up without Novocain, because it wouldn't do any good. He tells me "Scream if you want to." It wasn't as bad as I thought, and he asked me at one point "How does it feel", and I replied "It feels like a needle going through my arm."

Then for some odd reason the nurse decides to tell me that my roommate will be the suicide case. The Doctor tells me she is just joking, and she laughs. I have no idea why she thought that would be funny, it wasn't.

After that procedure of putting the flesh back together on my arm, I thought, as far as my arm was concerned, that the worst was over. That did not end up being the case.

Somewhere between the ER and my room I notice Anne, John Seniors wife. John must have realized it was more serious than he let on. Anne tells me that John sent her up to make sure I was ok, and that he would be up to see me in the morning.

Back at St Mary's Hospital, Bill and Mary have been waiting a long time in the emergency room. Mary is thinking I must be DOA, because too much time has passed. When she approaches the desk to ask about my condition, the nurse tells her that I was taken to the Methodist Hospital.

When Bill and Mary arrive, they find me in my room with Anne sitting next to the bed. I tell them that I'm fine. Although Mary later says "You didn't look good to me at all!"

After visiting hours, I lay in bed watching the band "Abba" on TV wondering, why I am here in the hospital. I felt great, I just didn't see the reason I should be there when I could be back home at Marks.

Sometime after midnight, I finally fell asleep. Certain that I would be released the next morning.

Chapter 9 – I told you I wouldn't get killed in that thing!

I woke up the next morning and found a mirror on the inside of the tray table next to my bed. When I looked at my face, I was shocked. It was a mess. My right eye was filled with blood, a result of taking off the rear view mirror on the way out of the car. My hair was also matted with blood, and my face was just overall bruised.

At this point, whatever medications they were putting into me, made me feel like absolute crap. The previous night I was ready to go home, today I felt absolutely horrible.

John Senior arrived sometime in the morning and I said to him "If only I hadn't taken that motorcycle ride, or had a bigger car." John looks at me and says "Ratter (his nickname for me since I was 10 years old), you can't go down that line of thinking. If you had a bigger car, maybe you would have been killed, you just can't think that way."

I get a phone call from my mom shortly after this, and she asks how I'm doing and then tells me that when I get discharged, my Aunt Agnes will take me in until they get home. She felt I was probably not going to be able to take care of myself. She was right about that, but I wasn't thrilled about being with Agnes or even being back with my parents.

Then my mom says "Your father wants to talk to you." Dad gets on the phone and asks how I am and I say "I told you I wouldn't get killed in that thing!" What followed was "Judas Priest" followed by some expletives and then Dad telling me that when he gets back home, I am going to be "driving the Buick LeSabre from now on." I respond "I don't think so."

After that call, I have a steady stream of visitors. Mark comes up at some point and takes some photos of me in my hospital bed. He tells me that he got some really good pictures of what's left of the beetle and says "John Boy, it's hard to believe anyone could have survived that wreck."

I keep wondering if Tammy knows I'm here, and if there is any possibility that she will make a visit. I felt that there was enough of a connection, that she would probably come and see me. However, Tammy had no idea how bad the accident was, and so it never happened. She later told me that if she had known I was in the hospital she would have come.

As more friends begin to come to the room, it begins to irritate my room-mate. So much so, that after he complains to the nurses, they end up moving me to another room. Here I meet my new room-mate Rodney, he had just had knee surgery.

I liked Rodney immediately because he is very talkative and just a funny sort of guy. Coincidently, he lived in Fort Atkinson.

Rodney wants to hear all about the accident. I fill him in on what I can remember of it. He tells me "Man, you are lucky to be alive."

At this point in the stay, all my nutrients are coming from the IV bag. I ask for food but am told that it will still be a day or two before that happens. So, I get to watch Rodney eat, and that's frustrating.

On day three the doctor came into my room and wanted to look at my arm and he unwrapped the bandages. I looked down and my arm was a mess (I won't go into detail…too graphic). The doctor turned to the nurse and said "It's not healing, we need to do a wet to dry." Then, without telling me anything about that procedure, he left the room.

I asked the nurse as she came back with some supplies "What is a wet to dry?" She explained that they are going to pour a solution on my arm and the bandages. It will harden and then they will "rip it off." I thought she was joking, because that sounded just entirely too primitive for a medical procedure.

The nurse applied the solution and the bandage. The burning was intense. She told me that "if it gets really bad" to use my call button. Some of the solution has just happened to roll down onto my back where the other wounds are located. Fifteen minutes later the pain there is pretty much unbearable, and I called for a nurse. It took two more calls over the next half an hour to get someone to come in and wipe down my back.

Two days later, the medical team came in and removed the dressing. The nurse had not been joking. It took three ripping motions to remove the dressing, and it was painful.

Rodney was sitting on the edge of his bed watching the whole procedure. I'm not watching the procedure; I'm watching Rodney. He's looking at my arm with an expression you would see on someone who watching a rocket launch; a weird blend of excitement, anticipation, and amazement.

After the last yank of the dressing, Rodney asks me "What does it feel like?" I tell him that "It feels like blood is just running down my arm." Rodney smiles and says "Oh, there is, there is a lot of blood running down your arm."

At some point in the next day or two they start to give me "somewhat solid food", starting with lime Jell-O. Even that horrible flavor tastes good after not eating for so long. Gradually I get more and more types of food added, and now I am feeling really quite good.

Boomer pays me a visit, and brings a gift from his mother, a box of homemade fudge with walnuts. It looked delicious, of course the nurse told me that "I couldn't eat that", so I just left it on my tray table.

Day six arrives and the nurse tells me that if I can produce a BM, well then the doctor will discharge me. She tells me that she will help things along with a suppository. I ask her to give me a minute, and she leaves the room.

I ask Rodney "What is a suppository?", and he smiles and pushes his index finger up into the air. "Ugh. That's what I thought."

When the nurse returns, I tell her that I really want to try to go to the bathroom without a suppository. She tells me "There is no way that you are going to be able to go without help, it's been too long, but go ahead and try, I'll be back."

What happens next is the best part of the whole hospital stay. I go into the bathroom but can only pass gas. I can hear Rodney in the other room laughing hysterically in between moments where he would ask "Any luck?" What ensued was hysterical laughter from both of us.

I finally came out and I said "No luck." However, then I had a brainstorm. I grabbed a piece of fudge and shaped it accordingly. It was a work of art. I tossed it into the toilet and got back into bed.

A short time later, the nurse returned and asked if I was ready, and I said "Nope, I went already, go check it out." At this point Rodney almost can't control himself.

She walks into our bathroom and exclaims "Oh good god", then she comes out and says "You didn't need to save that, I would have taken your word" and she starts to leave. Then Rodney yells out "It's fudge!" I'm sure he was only thinking of what was best for me, but now the jig was up. However, I was able to convince the nurse to let me administer the medication myself. She turned to me when she left and said "Now I am going to have you save it, and no fudge!" Rodney assures her that he will be watching me closely.

I asked Rodney a few minutes later how I would know when it was going to work. He said "Don't worry…you'll know."

I was discharged a few hours later.

Chapter 10 – Road to Recovery and a Wedding.

It was a longer than expected recovery. It took about six weeks to get released for work again. Even then I couldn't do any heavy lifting. So, John Senior's son Johnny acted as my arms for a couple of weeks while I eased back into the grind.

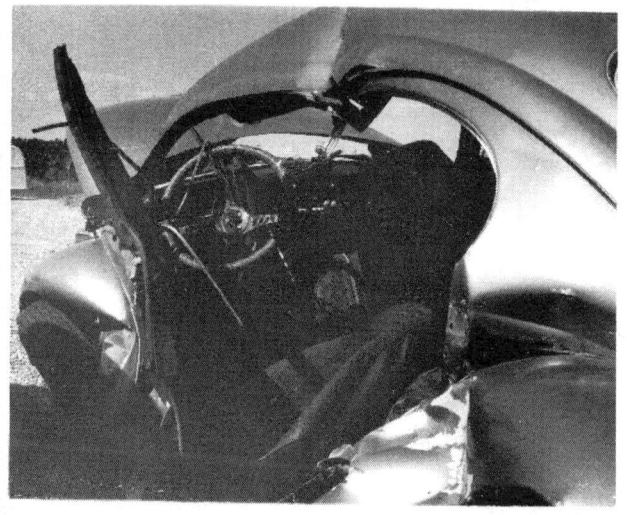

My roommate Mark eventually took me to the junk yard in Wyocena Wisconsin that housed the remnants of my 66 beetle. It was depressing. It sat off in the corner of the junk yard, open to the elements. I looked in the back where my trench coat always lay, but it was gone along with the tape recorder.

Now my little brown bear would end up being just another parts car. Probably the only thing worth taking would be the engine and transmission. Nothing else was really salvageable.

Shortly after this, Dad and Mom returned from Washington, and Dad and took me car shopping. He said "It's time to get back on the horse." Of course, you could be sure it wasn't a VW dealership we were going to. We ended up at Jon Lancaster Chevrolet when they were located in downtown Sun Prairie.

We found a brand new 1976 Chevette. Although it was not a bug, it did have a manual transmission. In many ways, it was basic transportation, just like the 66 had been. Everything was manual, no air conditioning, no power windows, nothing extravagant. However, I did really like it. A few years later the Chevette would be referred to as the Volkswagen Beetle of America when it became the best-selling small car.

Dad negotiated the deal, and I signed the papers. I was on the road again. Who would have thought when I had looked at Boomers Gremlin a little over a year earlier and wondered "when will I get a new car", that history would unfold this way.

It was now approaching fall, and my desire to drive to and from Fort Atkinson for work was waning. I loved seeing Tammy each day, but for the money I was making and the miles I was putting on the new car, it just didn't make sense. I struggled over what to do over the next couple of months and then decided to resign. I was sure I could find work in Madison. Maybe, just maybe, I'd get the nerve to ask Tammy out on a date before I left.

A couple of times I drove around her neighborhood hoping that she would be walking home from school, so I could offer her a ride. I never got lucky enough to find her. Although, she told me much later that she had seen me drive by her house once.

On the last day at work Tammy actually approached me about coming to her house for dinner that night. I had to be in Madison to meet with my dad and the insurance folks that particular night, so for that reason, and the fact that I looked absolutely horrible that day, I had to say no.

I certainly wasn't going to meet her parents in a one-piece ink covered jump suit.

Even after this, I was still afraid to ask her out. If she said "No", that would be humiliating, but at least I wouldn't need to face her at work each day.

I finally got up the nerve to call her a week later and ask her out. I forgot that the next Friday was New Year's Eve, and when I realized that during our phone call I said "Oh, next Friday is New Year's Eve, you probably already have a date." She said that she didn't and that I could pick her up at 5:00 on New Year's Eve. I was stoked. I had been infatuated with her since the very first time I saw her. Now, hopefully our date would go as well as the flirting at the postage machine.

The week sped by and Friday was rapidly approaching. Having shared the news with my brother Bill; he said "Yeah, you better go get some decent clothes for your first date." So, off we went to the mall to pick out some new jeans, and a nice shirt.

When Friday the 31st came I was a little more than excited. I had made reservations at my favorite restaurant, Nino's Steak House. After that we would go to the movie, A Star is Born.

I got to Tammy's house a little early and stood awkwardly in the kitchen waiting for her. I expected to meet her dad on this visit, but that would be at a later date. He was an over the road truck driver, and he wasn't home yet.

Once Tammy came into the room, her mom said "Why don't you show John the Christmas Tree." Tammy sort of rolled her eyes and then led me into their front room. I will say one thing for Tammy's mom, she sure knows how to decorate a tree. It was covered in small blue lights and ornaments; it really was beautiful. After that we said our goodbyes and left for Madison.

Once we were on the road, any thoughts of the date not going well for the most part evaporated. We had a great time at dinner and the movie.

We actually missed the first ten minutes of the movie since we arrived a bit late. So, we watched it a second time, which coincidentally ended a few minutes before midnight. I asked her as we stood up "Do I get a new year's kiss?" She responded with "It's not midnight…yet." I waited until midnight and got my kiss. Best kiss ever!

Forty minutes later I dropped Tammy off at her front door and asked if she wanted to go out the next weekend; she did.

What started next was an incredible amount of time driving between Fort Atkinson and Madison. I was driving more to see Tammy than I would have if I would just have kept working there.

Meanwhile over the next six months, things were taking a darker turn at home. The person that hit me in the intersection and totaled my 1966 beetle, began to harass me. It started on the phone, with him thinking I could somehow help him get his driver's license back. Obviously, to someone sane, which he was not, he would realize I had no power over the Department of Transportation.

Even if I could have helped, I would not have. This guy was a menace on the road, and he was a menace in his personal life. He had a police record for lewd and lascivious behavior that was a mile long. Suffice it to say he was a very unstable sort of guy.

A few days before Valentine's Day of 1977, he appeared at my front door on Waubesa Street. I have no idea how he knew where I lived. Perhaps he got the information from the accident report. He started complaining again about his driver's license. I had pretty much reached my breaking point now. I stepped out on the porch, and he began backing down the steps. He could see I was not afraid.

"How did you get here today?" I asked. He pointed at my Chevette and said "You're driving your new car, and I'm driving mine", then he turned and left.

I immediately went in the house and called the police department. When they arrived, they already knew plenty about him. The officer said, "If I were you, I would have a baseball bat or something handy…just in case he comes back." They told me that they would follow up but that he was probably already home, and would deny having been at my place.

So, now it is Saturday morning, Valentine's Day of 1977. I go out to my car with a gift for Tammy and turn on the ignition and try to pull away from the curb. The car won't budge. I get out thinking maybe the car's tires had frozen in the ice overnight. Instead, I find that every tire is flat. Each one had multiple large knife cuts in them.

It's another call to the police who immediately send detectives to his house. This time their intervention seems to have an impact as I never hear from him again.

Back on the home front, behind my back, my brother was talking about vigilante justice for the perpetrator of the accident. He and a few of his friends thought it might be time to pay the guy a visit. My dad quickly stifled any talk of retribution.

In my neighborhood there was also active talk of vigilante justice. Mark had shared with the neighbors what had happened, and Jose called me over to his front porch.

"I want you to know, we (as he pointed up and down the street) are all looking out for you. We are going to be watching for this guy, and we are going to make sure you are safe. If this guy shows up around here, we aren't waiting for the police, we are going to deal with this."

What can you say to that? It was rather overwhelming to know that my neighbors were so concerned about me. I felt very safe.

Later a flatbed trailer hauled my car away to get new tires, and I called Tammy and filled her in on what took place. From that point forward Tammy and I continue to date without any more bad history following me.

Nineteen months after our first date, on July 2nd, we were standing on the alter in the United Methodist Church in Fort Atkinson. The Chevette had been decorated by Boomer who had created a large "Just Married" sign that almost filled the back window on the hatch back.

The Chevette was Tammy's car now. I had purchased a 1973 Chevy truck in March; and that was a huge mistake. It was fun to drive, but got about 5 miles per gallon in the city. I traded the truck in at Bruns VW, two months later for the

only used bug they had on the lot at the time, a
1972 super Beetle. Had there been an available
1966 model, that would have been the choice.

Obviously, my dad thought I was crazy, but I
just couldn't get over the loss of my 1966 beetle.
"I can't believe you bought another one of those
cars, are you crazy?" I looked at Dad and replied
"Really Dad, what are the odds of being in another
car accident like that again?" Bill who was
standing nearby said, "Yeah, that's probably
true…that would be freak, like getting hit by
lightning twice; what are the odds of that ever
happening again?" Dad just shook his head,
murmured something and walked away.

The 1972 Super Beetle outside my parent's house.

There were some improvements that were
made between 1966 and 1972 for sure. Namely, a
larger engine with a 12-volt system. Also, there
was an electric powered defroster on the

windshield. Lastly, I wouldn't need to open the trunk to fill the car with gas.

Mechanically, this bug was as sound as they come. I put an incredible amount of mileage on the bug. I used it every day for school and work.

My first couple of years at the university I would park in a lot far off campus, and then bicycle into my classes. A cool little bike rack fit cleverly on the rear engine deck lid.

Later as the classes for my major were located closer together, I would park on the street. Tammy, who was working nearby, would move my car during the day to the opposite side of the street; so that I wouldn't get a parking ticket.

The beetle also made occasional trips to Oconto, so that we could repair my grandma's house which my parents had taken ownership of.

I was religious in my oil changes, tune ups, and valve adjustments. So much so, that I now was performing valve adjustments for other VW owners where I worked, and some tune-ups on American cars.

Once when I was at Bruns Volkswagen picking up some parts, I had a conversation with the service manager about VW repair. After about ten minutes of talking, he offered me a job. I asked him what the hourly pay was going to be and he educated me on "Book Rate." He then described that if a repair job is listed in the Volkswagen service manual as a two-hour job, and the service technician takes one hour to complete the job, they would be paid for two hours' worth of work. However, if it took longer than that, the pay is only for two hours. That would be fine if all I performed was oil changes, valve adjustments, and tune ups. However, there was a lot I didn't know that would put me at a real disadvantage.

That kind of structure did not appeal to me, so I declined the offer. I needed something more stable than getting paid "by the job."

Dennis and I were now working together and going to the university at the same time. We attended school during the day, and then worked second shift at a local meat plant, performing sanitation.

Dennis, who owned a 72 beetle, came into work one afternoon and announced that he had just bought a 1963 VW Beetle.

I went outside to look at it. It was that nice pearl white color, and looked to be in nice shape. Dennis said after driving it, he thought it might need work. We took it for a short drive, and as we cruised down the street, I could see the expression on Dennis's face turn into a depressing frown.

"Yeah, somethings not right with it" I said. "Maybe it's something simple, but you'll need to take it somewhere." Dennis was depressed the rest of the night, but shortly thereafter he got that little bug running nicely. His 1963 was a beautiful car.

Months later, after an engine failure that was the result of a mechanic leaving a rag in his oil pan, he found an old-world German mechanic named Ernie. Ernie would be Dennis's mechanic from then on, until he left Madison for Grad School, along with his 63 beetle.

In my junior year of college, I realized the 1972 needed some serious body work, because the rust was taking over the bug. A smarter twenty-year-old would have either 1) found a reputable body shop, or 2) just trade it in for a newer bug. I did neither of those.

Dennis was facing the same rust issues at the time. Together we ended up at a body shop on the east side of Madison, that totally misrepresented the type of work they could do. They actually did a decent job on Dennis's 63 beetle. On mine, well it was horrible. I ended up taking them to small claims court, and won. From then on, I just had no intention of throwing any money at the body of the super beetle.

Chapter 11 – Something just doesn't look right.

It's now 1982, and Tammy and I have had our first child, Jennifer. She was born about a month before I graduated from college.

My brother insisted that we use his car while he was traveling on business, he did not want his new niece coming home from the hospital in a Chevette, or worse yet a beetle.

Needless to say, I would never have put Jennifer in the beetle. However, the Chevette was a pretty safe vehicle. We appreciated the use of Bill's car and got Jennifer home safely.

Fortunately for us, the first night home excluded, Jennifer was a wonderful baby. A better natured baby you would never find.

As I mentioned before, during this period there were trips to Oconto to work on the house. I got involved late in the project and it was a learning experience for sure.

Prior to Jennifer being born, Tammy, Bill, Mary, and her boyfriend at the time, Gerry, and I would go up north and work on the house together. A year or so later, Gerry and Mary were no longer an item, and we were then joined by Marys' new boyfriend Jose. Jose and I bonded quickly and we took trips up north to work on the house together. A book could easily be written about all the adventures and misadventures working on this house.

On one of our trips at the house, we found a handy man who we thought could perhaps help us with some things like a stair rail to the second story. We found out shortly after talking to him, that he knew my mother. Instead of saying something you might expect, he tells us "I never seen a better set of teeth on a woman." This is why I say I could write a book about that place. There is a lot more where that came from.

Well, one weekend I asked Dennis if he wanted to go up north and help me do some re-siding of the north facing wall. Dennis was game so we loaded up the 72 super beetle and were on our way.

The weather was great for doing outside work, and we made great progress that weekend. We got a fair amount of siding scraped, replaced, and painted.

Sunday morning came and we locked up the house and walked towards the beetle, which was parked on the street. I looked at the front end and I said to Dennis "Look at the grill, something just doesn't look right." Dennis being a beetle, not a super beetle owner at the time, replies "I don't see anything wrong with it."

There is a grill just behind the front bumper. I could clearly see that whatever was directly behind it, had dropped a few inches lower than the grill. I was concerned because my 72 super beetle had turned into a pretty good rust trap by now.

Well, this was perhaps damage caused by the accumulation of ten years of Wisconsin rain, snow, and salt. Worse yet, perhaps it was the front end falling apart. I didn't want another railroad episode.

I knew the car was losing its battle against time my senior year in college. A horrible storm had moved across Wisconsin, and hit Madison the hardest. The rain had poured all morning, and it was torrential. To make matters worse, I had a final exam to take that day.

As I made my way towards campus, I could see cars pulled over to the side of the road just prior to a large intersection that was filled with water. A semi went through the intersection which now looked like a small lake. Water came halfway up his tires. I thought, "Well if I get a good running start, I bet I can make it."

I throttled up the engine and hit the water. I made some headway at first while keeping the engine running at a high RPM. Then the rear wheels came off the pavement, I was floating towards the other side of the road. Meanwhile water was pouring into the car from the floor's heater vents. It wasn't a slow leak either, it was shooting into the car as if it was under pressure. This was a sign that the heater channels were completely rotted through.

Suddenly I felt the rear wheels connect with the pavement. The beetle and I bobbed up and down violently several times, and then I was on the road driving again. So, I knew this wasn't a solid car, not anymore.

Later that afternoon I used a paper cup to bail out what water was left in the front and rear seat floor areas.

A few months later I tried to put a new heater cable into the beetle. There is a little round tube the cable is threaded through to get to the rear of the beetle where it is hooked up. That tube must have been full of rust because I couldn't get the new cable to go all the way in. My solution was to just drive the car with the cable as far in the tube as it would go, and then hope enough vibration would get it past the problem area. After a few rides, the cable made it all the way to the back of the car. All of this was of course an omen.

On the way into the downtown area of Oconto, there was a gas station/auto repair shop. I turned to Dennis and said "Let's see if anyone here can figure out what the issue with the bug is. I don't feel good about taking it on the highway." Dennis agreed and we pulled into the front of the service area.

The service technician raised my '72 super beetle on the hoist and walked underneath it. Then he came out and told me "I don't know much about beetles but I think it looks fine."

To me, that was at least a green light to get on the road to Madison, but I knew Monday morning I would be at the Bruns Volkswagen service department, because I knew something was just not right.

After the Oconto trip, I told Tammy I had a bad feeling about the bug. Of course, the next morning, I was the first person at the door of Bruns

VW. I told them something didn't look right with the front end of the bug, and that I thought maybe the MacPherson Strutt front end needed a rebuild.

About a half an hour later the service advisor said "Your frame head is completely rotted off; you shouldn't even be driving this beetle."

"Well can you fix it?" I asked.

"I don't know, it would depend on whether we could find any good metal under there" he replied. Even I knew this was probably not a possibility.

"Forget it…I'm going to do something else"

This was devastating news for a couple of reasons, the first being that Tammy and I just had Jennifer, and money was tight. I absolutely didn't need a new car payment. Secondly, this car had seen me through college, and had never cost me any money outside of the oil I bought.

After I left Bruns, I drove immediately and in a somewhat paranoid manner to Jon Lancaster Chevrolet and negotiated a deal on a brand new four door Chevette. I can't remember what they gave me for the bug, but anything was probably more than it was worth at that point.

I have since watched some videos on frame head replacement on a super beetle. To do it correctly, the body of the beetle would need to be removed. Obviously with as much rust as this beetle had, there would be no point in doing a ground up restoration on it. Sometimes you just need to know when you are facing a losing battle.

I went over to my folks house the next morning early and said to my dad "My beetles shot, the frame head is rotted off and it's not safe to drive anymore...I just took out a new car loan, and I don't think I'll need any help with the payments but if something happens down the road, can I float a loan from you to make a payment?"

Dad, obviously thrilled that my beetle was on the way to the junk yard answered "Of course!" The last thing he wanted was me or anyone in my family, especially Jennifer, near that beetle.

I never did need help to make the payments, but as I mentioned, the need for a car came at a very inopportune time in our lives.

The 1976 Chevette had been a really good car, so hopefully the '82 four door Chevette would be equally good. Although it was six years newer than the '76, it was still just good basic transportation.

From this point forward for the next twenty years, I often looked on and off to see if any beetles were for sale in Wisconsin. Keep in mind, this is prior to the advent of the internet. This meant that searching was just reading the local newspaper classified section. However, two things were happening during this period of time:

One, Wisconsin, and really, anywhere in the northern states, destroys vehicles with their winters. The salt on the roads would rust out the heater channels, the seams between the fenders, front light buckets, and the floor pans. If I were going get a 1966 beetle again, it would need to be solid. I wasn't interested in anything that was compromised.

Two, Madison, which had at one time been home to so many beetles, was now pretty much bare of them. This was probably due to number one, above.

So, during this period my searching stalled out, our family grew, and we moved twice due to my new job.

My in-laws Helen, and Jerry also knew of my love for the beetle, and would occasionally tease me with "There's a beetle for sale out on highway 106. We saw it when we went shopping the other day." Helen would have seen my original 66 back in 1976 when she dropped Tammy off for work. Helen and Jerry were both familiar with my 72-super beetle. They probably would have gotten a kick out of it, had I found another one, but as I mentioned, anything available in Wisconsin would be in pretty rough shape.

Then shortly after the year 2000, Tammy and I took a trip to Cozumel, Mexico. One morning we rented an old Volkswagen beetle to drive around the island. It was an absolute piece of junk. The throttle cable needed to be replaced, the steering and brakes needed work, and it sounded like it was going to fall apart over every bump in the road. It did, however, light a fire in me.

Chapter 12 – Be careful what you wish for.

Shortly after our return from Cozumel, I began looking in earnest for a 1966 beetle. It was a difficult search.

Even though the internet was full of sites that had vehicles for sale, the odds of finding a solid 1966 seemed challenging if not impossible.

I began looking at a site I had stumbled upon by freak chance, thesamba.com. This site had an enormous classified section. However, almost all of the 1966 models were, for the most part, in horrible shape. I did not want a project car.

Then I stumbled onto a gentleman who was doing a bottom-up restoration in Georgia to a couple of 1966 beetles. He sent me some pictures of the cars and said I could pick the paint color if I wanted one.

I thought it over for a few days, and then I contacted him and told him I was interested, and the paint should be the stock 1966 VW color called Sea Sand.

The reason I chose Sea Sand, is that I thought it would be the closest color to what I had on my original beetle. While Sea Sand isn't even close to the "goldish" color of the first '66, it can take on a gold type look depending on the sun and angle you are viewing it. In addition, I wanted a stock 66 color, and Sea Sand fit the bill.

Body Work on the 1966 Sea Sand Beetle.

He began sending me regular pictures of the beetle as it progressed through the body work part of the processes.

This guy really did a nice job on the body work, but as I would find out he was a shyster when it came to mechanical work. He absolutely lied about his expertise in that area, or perhaps he just decided to do a very substandard job on my beetle.

He delivered the beetle to us very late one evening. I wrote him a check for the balance after

The 1966 body work underway.

listening to it run and seeing him drive it down the street before pulling into my driveway. By the time I had taken it for a short ride, he had already beat feet out of our subdivision. That was the first indication that I was in trouble. The second indication was that the transmission would disengage in second gear.

I called him the next day and he said he would reimburse me for any expense related to the transmission. After that call he changed his phone number, and ghosted me. Later I found another site where someone had delt with him on an airplane and also came up short.

It was now up to me to fix the beetle. It wasn't 1975 anymore, and the number of shops that knew how to work on beetles were infinitesimally small.

I eventually found a classic Volkswagen repair facility in Milwaukee. They confirmed that the transmission was bad and they replaced mine with one they had rebuilt. The rebuilt one ended up being just as bad as the original, so they put a second transmission in, at their expense.

Now we are approaching Christmas. It's not Christmas of 1975 again, but it might as well be. Jennifer and I decided that we would take my 1966 beetle from our house in Pleasant Prairie, to Madison, then to Fort Atkinson, to drop off Christmas gifts to our families.

Somewhere between Madison and Fort Atkinson, the engine began to lose power. It becomes a very creepy de-ja-vu. As I pull up to my sister in-laws house to drop off presents, I refused to turn the car off. Mainly because I was afraid that I wouldn't be able to get it to start again. That would be about the worst possible scenario I could think of.

Jennifer sat in the car as my brother-in-law Dick came to the door. We talked for just a few seconds and I told him I needed to get going because the bug is "running like shit!" He craned his head around me to look at his driveway. "It's a 66 beetle" I say "and somethings not right."

So off we go, Jennifer and I cruise unhappily along on our way back to Pleasant Prairie. On the way home I anxiously wait to hear the dreaded trash can noise behind the car, as a valve shoots through the engine case. Fortunately, for me, that never happens. We continue to cruise at about 50 miles per hour, it was the most I could get out of my bug; but we made it home.

Now, I was really frustrated. I was not going to take the car back to Milwaukee, because I didn't trust them anymore after two transmissions. So, another search began. After a day or so of searching, I found a real gem; Burlington Import Auto.

Burlington Import Auto was owned by Terry and Gary. Both guys were about my age, and I knew immediately in talking with Terry, that he was going to be "My Guy."

Tammy followed me out to the Burlington shop. I'm sure at this point she was thinking her main purpose in life was to drop me and the '66 off at various VW repair shops.

After I told Terry about what I was experiencing with the engine he said "Give me a day to look it over, and I'll give you a call." With that we departed. I knew, without a doubt, Terry would find the solution to the hell that I had made for myself.

The next day Terry called me. "I had to tear the engine apart. Whoever rebuilt this engine did a pretty good job until they put in bad valve springs." Well, now I knew I was in for an engine rebuild. "Let me ask you something, I know you want this to be as original as possible, but it doesn't have the original engine in it, it's not a six-volt system, and it's not the original color, so let me drop a 1600 engine into it. You'll get more power and better cooling with a dual port engine. Trust me, you will be happier." At this point being happier sounded like a good idea. "Sure Terry..go ahead" I responded. "Good move" he said "Come pick it up next weekend."

When Tammy took me back to Burlington Import, I could see my Sea Sand beetle behind the locked fence. Terry talked to me about the break-in period and when I was supposed to bring it back for its first valve adjustment and oil change. We walked out to where the bug was parked, and it fired right up. It sounded wonderful.

Terry and Gary's mechanical work was everything I had thought it would be and more, it was perfect. Driving the bug home was a real pleasure. Once I got home Tammy and I took it for a short drive and then I parked it in the garage for the weekend. I didn't want to risk getting road salt all over the new paint with a snow storm now approaching our area of Wisconsin.

After that storm, but before the roads were cleared and salted, I took the 66 out in the snow, and drove towards Kenosha. It brought back wonderful memories of the "little brown bear" sliding over snow drifts.

As spring emerged, I began taking it to work regularly. As I mentioned, the color Sea Sand is unusual. I would get comments like, "I saw your (insert color here: beige, clay, gold, or sand colored) beetle in the lot."

I would always say "It's called sea sand, but I know it looks different depending on the lighting." I loved that paint, it was, and remains, one of my all-time favorite colors.

The 66 Seas Sand Beetle, at the Kenosha Harbor.

I was now extremely proud of my 66 beetle. In retrospect what I initially spent on it was probably reasonable given the ground up restoration, even with a bad engine. There was no crying over spilled milk, I just needed to move on.

I was ready for something big now, a road trip to see Dennis. That would be ambitious because of the distance and because there was no radio, just the sound of the engine. It would be 877 miles of just me and the 66, from Wisconsin through Indiana, Ohio, Pennsylvania, New Jersey, then into New York.

Mapping out the drive was reminiscent of planning the beetle ride west with Johnny as a kid. However, much had changed since then.

After a call to Dennis, I put my plan into action starting with a visit to Terry's shop to go through the beetle and make sure all systems were good to go, and they were.

The folks at work told me I was crazy to drive to New York in the beetle. One of my staff said, "I can't believe you're going to spend that much time in the bug with no radio…you're going to go nuts after just a few hours." He obviously did not understand that classic beetle owners love the sound of that engine. I really didn't worry about not having the radio, with the exception of getting a weather forecast.

The next week was the first week in April, and I left for New York. My plan was to make the drive in one day. So I left the house in Pleasant Prairie about two in the morning giving Tammy and the puppies a kiss before I left. I was really excited to make the trip and see Dennis.

Chapter 13 – Cohoes, New York

The first two hours were made up of just getting around Chicago. The earlier you get around Chicago the better. It was about 3:00 AM as I cruised by the downtown area. It really is a beautiful city at night, with all the buildings illuminating the darkness.

Once I was past Chicago, it was on to Indiana, and then Ohio. Ohio became a very boring drive, with very little to see. It was much flatter than I had pictured. The beetle hummed along wonderfully mile after mile. Occasionally I would be passed by cars where the driver or passenger would give me a "thumbs up." With the exception of gas stops, I never left the beetle.

Part way through Ohio, I noticed rain drops on the windshield. What initially looked like a very sunny day had started to change to an overcast drizzle. After a short time, I turned on the wipers. They worked alright, but there was definitely a certain amount of shaking that they would make. I wasn't overly concerned about this; it would just be something I would need to deal with when I got to Dennis's house.

Entering Ohio on the way to New York.

The rain stopped on the far side of Ohio and then it just became a beautiful drive. I was getting about 30 miles to the gallon, but of course it's a small gas tank so I would fill up with gas about every 200 miles, just to be safe. The main reason to fill up so often was because the gas gauge is based on a float inside the tank. The needle moves up and down as you drive, more so when you stop and start. I didn't want to risk running out of gas, so I played it safe.

About four in the afternoon, I was getting very close to Cohoes. After a little confusion on which exit to take, I ended up parked in front of

Dennis's house. The 66 was probably thankful for the rest stop.

After Dennis and I spent some time together I called Wolfsburg West and ordered some windshield wiper shafts, and bushings. When they arrived a few days later, Dennis supervised me as I hung over the side of the bug to replace the parts. It ended up not making much of a difference, but it was a bit better.

We went to dinner at a steak place the first night. It was great. It was a nice thirty-minute ride back to highway 87 and then over the Mohawk River bridge. On the ride, Dennis was trying to calculate how long it had been since he had ridden in a beetle.

The next day we decided to drive about fifteen miles into Albany to visit the 911 exhibit at the New York State Museum. The Museum contains the largest and most comprehensive collection of artifacts related to the September 11 terrorist attack. Although we were three years removed from that horrible day at this point, it didn't feel like it at all.

A small part of the 911 exhibit.

After touring the museum, we walked back to the beetle, which was parked across the street from the State Capital Building.

The 66 beetle outside the State Capital building.

After we got back, Dennis and I relaxed for a while as his bunny (named appropriately Bun Bun) frolicked around the house. I am usually well-liked by everyone's pets, but his bunny never really warmed up to me at all.

The next day we were invited to Dennis's parents house for lunch. They were not very far away, so I doubt the beetle even got warmed up on that drive.

Their house was built by Dennis's dad. It was a large ranch log cabin on a nice piece of property.

Knowing how Dennis was, I was interested to see what kind of stock bred this individual. I thought his dad would probably be just as entertaining as Dennis.

What greeted us at the door was a hulk of a man with a powerful grip as he shook my hand. "Ralph Trumble" He stated "Hi Mr. Trumble, John Patterson" I responded.

Any of the expectations I had in parents for Dennis were completely wrong. Ralph was a very no non-sense, non-joking, sort of guy but genuinely warm and a good conversationalist. Dennis's mother was on the quiet side but very pleasant.

This could mean only one thing; Dennis had to be adopted. Certainly, his real parents were living in or near an asylum somewhere. How could someone as funny as Dennis come from this family? I suppose the same thing could have been said about my upbringing as well.

After a wonderful meal we were back to Dennis's house and his bunny

The next morning we drove to meet up with Gary, Dennis's brother. Gary apparently knew well in advance that I was coming, as he had made up a VW pendant, that looked somewhat like the color of my bug, and gave it to me. I was impressed. There was definitely a lot of talent in the Trumble lineage.

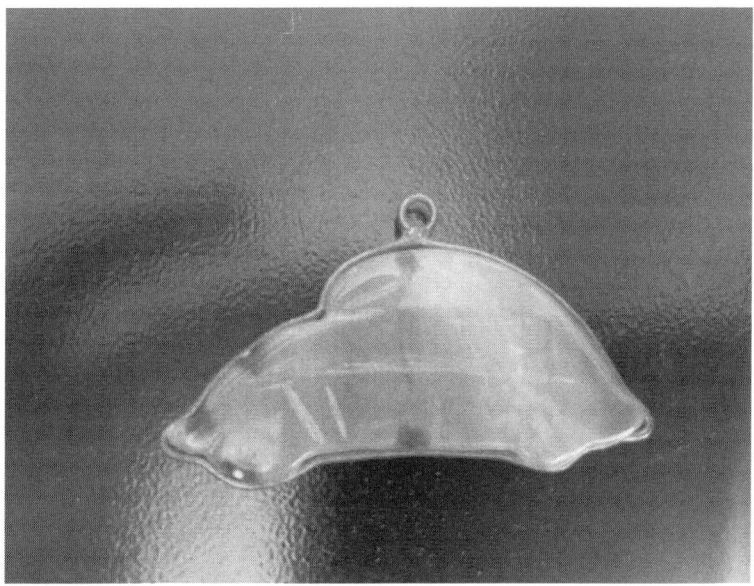

Gary's handiwork.

Gary gave us a tour of his little workshop and we chatted for about an hour or so. Then we were off again in the bug.

One thing that was rather momentous when I was in New York, was the fact that my newly refurbished speedometer turned over to 1966 miles. Three miles before that I took a picture for Dennis of it turning to 1963.

All too soon this vacation in New York was over and it was time to head back to Wisconsin. This had been the longest trip I had taken in a 1966 beetle, and it had performed better than I could have imagined.

Later that year I began creating a website just for 1966 VW beetle owners; 1966vwbeetle.com. I had hoped to get a couple dozen owners to join but before long I was pushing five hundred, and later over one thousand members.

The site has a forum so folks can talk about their bugs and share mechanical tips and information. I had no idea at the time that it would become so popular. In order to keep the database clean, I had to have a rule; if you don't post within the first year of joining, you get deleted from the forum; however, you can always re-join. If you make even one post, even just to introduce yourself and your car, you are on the forum for life.

Chapter 14 – Something more original

After the New York trip, Tammy and I began going to VW Car Shows. Although my bug would never place, it received some very nice comments.

The reason it never took any awards was primarily because it just wasn't original enough. This is a fact I knew all to well. The fenders, bumpers, floor pans, were all aftermarket parts. Anyone who judged beetles, knew that the engine wasn't true to the year of the car either. It was a beautiful car, but I began to want an original 1966 beetle.

So thus began my final search for a stock 1966. My search criteria would be as follows:

1)   Not a restoration
2)   Original Engine
3)   6 Volt System
4)   Original Color
5)   No Rust, and solid floor pans

Now you might think that would be an impossible task, well, so did I. In particular I worried that I wouldn't be able to find a 66 with an original engine.

When my search started, I was talking to Terry at his Burlington shop and he tried to sway me from getting another 66 beetle, especially an original model.

"Why on earth would you want that? Think for a minute, all you need to do is step up to a 1967 and you have a twelve-volt system and a better engine. There's hardly any difference between a 1966 and a 1967. The 67 would be better for you."

Terry was right about all of those things, but that's like telling someone that likes German shepherds, that they should get an Australian shepherd. After all they are both shepherds, and great family dogs. While that is completely true, they are not similar at all.

Besides being John Muir's favorite VW beetle, there were many things that made the 1966 model year unique.

1. It had the one year only 1300 beetle engine.
2. The dashboard was unchanged with the exception of a center mounted defroster vent.
3. New slotted wheels were introduced in order to aid in cooling of the brakes.
4. A new flat hub cap was introduced.

5. The windshield wipers now parked to the left side of the windshield.
6. A new locking mechanism on the seats prevented them from tipping forward during an accident.
7. The front axel was now ball joint vs. link and king pin.
8. The torsion leaf springs increased from eight springs to ten.
9. The emergency flasher is mounted on the dashboard.
10. The headlight dimmer switch was moved from the floor to the rear of the turn signal lever.
11. The half circle horn ring was reintroduced for the 66-model year.
12. A larger rear-view mirror was added.

I told Terry, "No, I don't want a '67', and he said "Yeah, you and your 1966 beetle thing, I know how you are…just think about it."

Of course, at this point my mind was made up and I began my search in earnest. Regardless of what I found, if it needed work, Terry would be the one to fix it.

I began searching in California and found a few reputable places that advertised beetles for sale. The beetles were represented with about fifty pictures covering everything from the engine to the spare tire wheel well. Every part of the car was displayed, including any flaws.

Then I found LaVere's VW, and contacted the owner, Gary, and told him what I was looking for. Gary told me that he knew someone who was trying to sell their 1966 beetle, and wanted to know if I wanted to get in touch with her. He told me that he had seen the beetle and it was about "as original as it gets, with the exception of the interior." He also mentioned that the paint on the roof had a small spot that was beginning to peel.

Gary explained that the owner, Mickey, was the second owner of the beetle. Her husband bought the car as just a fun little toy for her. He had since passed away and she was trying to sell some of the cars she felt she no longer needed. The beetle, which she drove very infrequently, was one that she wanted to sell.

The beetle's interior had at some point been redone to a grey velour along with a mohair headliner. "Actually, it looks pretty nice" Gary said. "Well, it sounds terrible, like something that was used in a porno movie, can you redo the interior back to the original?" "Absolutely" he laughed "but it will be expensive."

To be quite frank, I wasn't at all worried about the cost, because I planned to sell the Sea Sand beetle to pay for the Sea Blue beetle. So, I told Gary to go ahead and get started, and I sent a check to Mickey for the beetle. It was July 28th, 2005, I now owned two 1966 beetles.

At this point, all that was left to accomplish was to hire a transportation company to haul the beetle from Concord California, to Pleasant Prairie, Wisconsin.

You might think that this is an easy task, but when you are as OCD about things as I am, well it takes a lot of research. I wanted to select the company with the best reviews possible.

I finally selected ABM Auto Transport out of Spring Grove, Illinois. The cost to deliver the beetle would be eight hundred dollars. When comparing their rates to other companies, it was comparable. Gary LaVere would handle the shipping on his end. He assured me that he would go over the car with a fine-tooth comb before the driver left his shop. This way, any damage that might happen in transit, would be the liability of the transportation company.

The new to me 1966 beetle arrived in August. The trucking company felt uncomfortable driving into the subdivision, since their rig was so long. The driver asked if I would meet him at a Truckstop about five miles from home, near the interstate. I hopped in my car and drove down to meet him.

After signing the papers, I fired up the car, which ran beautifully, and headed for home. The first thing I noticed is that this car was solid, I mean really solid, just like my first 66. When I

The first picture of the new 66 beetle.

went over the railroad tracks in the small town of Russell, it was as if I was in a new car.

I got home and rolled up into the front yard and began taking pictures. It was beautiful, I couldn't have been any happier.

When Tammy came home, I think she was just happy it was a decent vehicle. At that point, she drove me back to the Truckstop to get my car. The sun was setting so there was only time for a quick tour of the interior of the Sea Blue bug, with a drive scheduled for after dinner.

Let me be clear about the six-volt system, it does the job, but as I mentioned before, it's a lot of demand on such a small system.

In addition, I wasn't 18 anymore. It was 30 years after my first 66, and that has to make a bit of a difference for driving at night in a six volt car.

We barely got out of the neighborhood when she turned to me and said "All right, I'm scared, take me home now." This was because as Terry would later say "That six volt system is like running in front of your car with candles at night." Well, that was exaggeration but now it was hard to imagine driving at night this way.

I turned to Tammy and said "Wow, if you said that in my first 66, I don't think there would have been a second date." She was offended "Well, back then I wouldn't have known any different so I would have been fine with it."

So we turned around and I dropped Tammy off at home and then I continued my short night time cruise.

I was really happy with the bug, but I was pretty sure that it would need to be repainted to get it back to its previous glory. Also, I wanted Terry to check out the paperwork I received from Mickey, because it had some engine work done to it. I wasn't sure after looking at the paperwork what had actually been done, but I knew Terry would be able to figure it out.

The next week I drove out to see Terry with the Sea Blue beetle and he looked at the paperwork. After a while he turned to me and said "There's not enough detail here to know exactly what they did to the engine." That wasn't good news, because having the original engine was important to me. I did not want to blow the original engine, and I did not know it's history.

I turned to Terry and I said "I think you should rebuild the engine, so we know it's ok." Terry looked at me and said "I know I'm not going to get anywhere arguing with you about this engine, and because this car is so original, I'm not even going to try...drop it off next week and we'll get started."

I left Terrys shop and drove directly to Perfection Autobody, also located in Burlington Wisconsin. Terry had recommended them if I was serious about repainting the car. Clayton, the owner, took me step by step through the process of what they would do to get the car looking great again. I was impressed at how much he understood about classic beetles and the way they were put together.

I got a quote from Clayton and scheduled the paint job. Once Terry finished the engine, he would drive it over to Clayton to get the paint job. Things were progressing nicely.

While the Sea Blue was getting its makeover, I was busy advertising the Sea Sand bug. At $5,500.00 I figured it would sell quickly, but it didn't. That fact didn't bother me too much, because we still had some car shows coming up

152

where I figured there would be a more interested audience.

It would be several months before the biggest VW Show, which was in Indianapolis, so I'd have both bugs at the same time for quite a while.

Yes, at this point I had two 1966 beetles, and a 2005 New Beetle convertible. The New Beetles were similar to the old beetles in shape only, and that is where the similarity ended.

Nothing screams obsession louder than two 1966 beetles and a New Beetle Convertible.

The new beetle was a great modern car. It had the engine in front, leather interior, heated seats, satellite radio, and a plethora of modern conveniences. It also got about thirty miles to the gallon, which was great for commuting. However, unlike the classic beetles, it was also <u>very hard</u> to work on. I had to replace a rear turn signal more than once, and getting the lens off to actually do that was an exercise in both frustration and profanity. Replacing the battery became a two-hour job while I loosened and removed engine parts that were in the way. Despite all this, it was a fun car.

Eventually the new 1966 was ready for pick-up at Clayton's shop. There she sat looking showroom perfect.

Chapter 15 – They appreciate it for what it is.

At this point Tammy and I started entering a lot of VW car shows. Some were close to home and some were not.

I liked showing the bug, not because of the awards that the Sea Blue Bug took, but because I finally had an all-original bug, and people appreciated it for what it was.

Almost every show had a cruise that followed the awards presentation. We both loved that part, because it was enjoyable to cruise the backroads with folks that shared your passion for VW's.

I now had one 1966 at home in the garage, and one beetle sitting in an outside storage one car garage. That storage facility was very secure, with a high locked fence, and someone on site during the day. I never worried about my 66 in that locked garage. However, the rent continued to increase there, and in a short time I was paying $200.00 a month. In addition, I was also paying another $125.00 a month at a different facility for storage of my travel trailer and motorcycle trailer.

The money at that point wasn't my primary concern. My main concern was now I owned things that were out of sight. There is something just a bit disconcerting when you have a lot of property you can't keep an eye on.

Also, there was a fair amount of jockeying going on. If I wanted to take the 1966 out of storage, I had three options. Either get a ride, drive a motorcycle over, or take my '05 new beetle. Then pull the 66 out and store the other vehicle. It just wasn't very convenient.

When we built the house in Pleasant Prairie in 2000, there was no neighborhood association. How one was established later, I have no idea, because we were never notified until it was already created. I would most certainly have voted against it.

I realize some neighborhoods probably are happy they have one. Our neighborhood didn't really need it. It became a thorn in our side, because we had poured a third pad for our travel trailer when we built, and now due to the neighborhood association, I couldn't utilize that third pad for the RV.

The rules were very restrictive, even when it came to loading and unloading the trailer for camping. Anyone who has an RV understands that it may take more than 24 hours to get loaded, and test your systems before getting on the road.

So, the third pad was primarily used now for the 66 beetles, but never in the winter. At least I got some use out of it.

The VW Website was also taking off, in a way that was hard to manage. I was getting many folks joining the forum and also getting a lot of spammers. A fair amount of time was being allocated to managing new registrations and writing code to block hacking attempts.

Now, when there were VW shows, Tammy and I were showing the Sea Blue 66, but our focus changed to taking the Sea Sand in hopes that someone might be interested in purchasing her.

There were two shows that I really enjoyed. One was "Volksbraten" in Sheboygan, Wisconsin. It was a nice show with great people, and was always in September. If I lived closer, I definitely would have joined their club. The second show was "Volktoberfest", in Brownsburg, Indiana. It was always in October.

As far as the show in Sheboygan, that was a short hour and a half drive. Once though, we decided to go up the night before the show and stay at a nearby motel.

Then we had a pleasant surprise. The last remaining Nino's Steak House was located in Sheboygan. Needless to say, that is where we went for dinner. While it wasn't the Nino's that we had gone to on our very first date, it was almost identical in décor; and the food was every bit as good. They would later close in 2011 after 41 years in business.

Volksbraten 2006.

The Sea Blue 66 always did well in Sheboygan, and we loved the food (brats of course), and the members couldn't be any nicer.

The Brownsburg "Volktoberfest" was completely different. It was huge, and the longer the day went, the larger it got. Tammy and I had been there a number of times and felt, perhaps it provided the largest number of potential buyers for the Sea Sand Bug. So, we left for Brownsburg in the Sea Sand Beetle.

Now, perhaps I should never have sold the Sea Sand 66, because it was a great running car, with a 12-volt system. I had grown attached to it because we had been through a lot if repairs to get her in great shape. However, how many cars can one guy own, and afford to insure and keep running?

Not running your VW Beetle on a regular basis is very bad for it. I found this fact out on vintage motorcycles that I had restored. Six beautiful Yamaha restorations from the 1970's that were impossible to keep running because there just wasn't enough time to ride all of them. That plus horrible ethanol in the gas, made carburetor rebuilding inevitable.

Realistically, another 1966 to take care of, store, and insure, just wasn't a great idea.

As we drove towards Brownsville that night, the rain came. At least I had a 12-volt system, so the wiper speed wasn't an issue. That was a good thing because this was almost a six-hour trip.

When I was a young driver, I enjoyed driving in the rain. As I got older, I enjoyed it less, primarily because of how reckless other drivers drove in slippery conditions. There was one other reason I wasn't fond of driving in the rain that night, it was dirtying up the beetle; a car I was hoping to sell.

About 10:00 PM Tammy and I checked into the hotel, and called it a night. I was hoping that tomorrow would be a dry and sunny day.

We got to the grounds of the show pretty early the next morning, and parked the bug. I placed a for sale placard on the windshield, washed her as best I could, while Tammy set up our lawn chairs at the rear of the bug.

My Girl Tammy and the Sea Sand Bug at Volktoberfest.

As I mentioned, this is a huge show. Even so, I thought the 66 was beautiful compared to others that were parking around us.

After a little while I saw a VW Van roll into the fair grounds that had a unique paint job. I believe it is called chameleon paint, and it changes color based on the angle you are viewing. It almost appeared to be tie-dyed. It was very cool to look at but nothing I would ever consider doing to a vintage vehicle.

Who wouldn't want to buy a nice Sea Sand 66?

Although the 66 Sea Sand beetle got a lot of attention, it seemed as though it would not be purchased that particular day. We both realized that was a possibility, but it was a little disappointing.

After the awards were presented at the show, the VW cruise began. This was my favorite part. They actually had the intersections controlled by local police so that we could stay together as a large group.

It was an absolutely beautiful day for a ride and I enjoyed the hour drive in the country.

The picture above, Tammy took while looking out the rear driver's side window back at the long string of beetles following us on the country cruise.

After the ride, we returned to the grounds, and began to get ready to head back to Wisconsin. Suddenly we were approached by the couple that owned the tie-dye van. They were interested in buying the Sea Sand Beetle. We talked price, shook hands, and then Tammy and I headed back to Wisconsin.

On the way home, I turned to Tammy and said "Gee, I hope they don't do that funky paint job on this beetle." She said "I know…but that's something you have no control over."

Six hours later we were home, the bug was put away, and we relaxed with our puppies.

The next Friday night we received a phone call from the folks in Indiana, they were just getting through Chicago traffic. They thought they would arrive at our place in about an hour.

When they pulled up in front of the house, I was shocked to see that they had towed a flatbed trailer behind them. As they approach us, I said "Wow, I thought you would just drive it home, it is totally road worthy!"

"Oh, I know" he replied, "it's not that, I just don't feel comfortable going through Chicago with the bug, too many crazy drivers."

I couldn't blame him for that, but it was pretty sad watching the Sea Sand get loaded on a flat bed trailer. The last time I saw it like that was the day it was delivered to me.

These folks weren't much for hanging around and talking, but they did have a long drive ahead, so I certainly understood. A few minutes later, they drove away with the Sea Sand bug, and faded away into the darkness of the neighborhood.

Now there was only one 66 beetle.

The next year we went to the Brownsburg show, but didn't see the tie-dye van anywhere. I had really hoped to see the 66 again, even if they had repainted it.

The Sea Blue 66 and the '05 New Beetle the next year.

We showed both the 1966 and the 2005 at the following years show. The 66 Sea Blue placed in their "Top 20" award, pretty impressive given the number of VWs at that show. The New Beetle didn't place, but it would later in the year at a different VW show, coming in third place in the new beetle – stock category. I think it would have come in first place if not for some speckling on the front hood, a result of rock salt getting kicked up on her during the winter.

Chapter 16 – It's Texas now.

There were a lot of shows that followed in the next few years. Surprisingly though, there was no VW Club in south east Wisconsin.

A gentleman approached me one day while I was fueling the Sea Blue 66 and asked if I wanted to start a VW club in Kenosha. I thought that was a great idea, so we planned to get together over the weekend and talk about it.

When we met later, I could see that his idea of a club differed radically from what I wanted. He wanted just a loose group of people, that could get together once and a while for a ride.

If I was going to get involved in a club, it was going to be regular monthly meetings, and a yearly car show. We didn't see eye to eye on anything we discussed but I told him if he wanted to organize rides, I would certainly tag along.

A couple of months later he called me and asked if I wanted to be in the fourth of July parade in Kenosha, along with some other VW owners. I said sure, then called my daughter and asked if she wanted to ride with me in the parade.

Jennifer is a teacher in Kenosha, and pretty outgoing so she said yes, and we made plans to get together at our house and then drive to the starting point of the parade.

The parade became less about the 66 and more about Jennifer. Many of her students began yelling to her along the route "Hey Miss Patty", this became a familiar refrain during the entire parade. We saw Tammy at some point along the route standing with our son Jeff and one of his friends.

Tammy takes this picture as we pass.

While we crept along the parade route, I became increasingly concerned about the ability of my engine to stay cool in this heat. It was mid

90's outside and very still. I wasn't just worried about the engine though; I was also worried about the clutch. On a parade route there is an incredible amount of clutching or feathering of the clutch, because you just start to move forward and then you need to stop again.

Looking forward as we drive the parade route.

The guy ahead of me in the line, had a Baja beetle. I'm a bug purist, so this is most definitely an aberration to me. To make matters worse, he had engineered it to generate as much noise as possible. It was like sitting behind a hot rod with glass packs at an intersection. Except this wasn't an intersection, it was a long route, and it was not an enjoyable experience.

I told Jennifer at one point, that between the heat and the Baja bug, I doubted I would sign up for this kind of torture again.

Miss Patty and the Sea Blue Parade Beetle.

When the parade was over, I spent no time hanging around. I wanted to get some air flowing over the engine of the 66 so I took off for home.

The next year Tammy and I took a vacation in Texas, and visited her sister, and brother-in-law. We thought Texas might be a good place to move to, when we eventually retired. In 2008 we purchased land northeast of Dallas.

I thought, this would be nice because, "You can drive the bug all year round in Texas." In addition, all my vintage motorcycles would be on the road all year too.

Our future property in Texas.

Moving to Texas would take another five years. Those were years filled with car shows, motorcycle restorations, more dogs joining the family, and Jennifer getting married.

Of course on and off, I would see Terry out at Burlington imports, sometimes for a valve adjustment, and other times just to drop in and see how he was doing.

There was one instance where my charging system was having issues and I went to see Terry. He had the car for a couple of days trying to figure out what the problem was. It turned out to be a bad voltage regulator, and when he replaced it, he ended up with a dud, so that one ended up being replaced as well.

It is hard to get quality parts for vintage Volkswagen beetles, and that's probably why he ended up with a bad voltage regulator. Sometimes a bad part just slips through, which must have been the case with the bad voltage regulator. Terry always tried to get the best possible parts. Believe me, he knew who manufactured junk; and he steered clear of it. As I mentioned though, you really couldn't get much of anything out of Germany.

Volkswagen gave up support for the beetle and its parts long ago. I have never understood why. VW really missed the boat on support for the Beetle, Ghia, Bus, Fastback, Squareback, and all the other VWs still out there. They could be making a fortune today in body panels alone, however, I bet they have relegated all the old classic beetle presses to the scrap yard years ago.

When I finally got out to the Burlington shop to pick up the car, I asked Terry what I owed him and he said "If I had to charge you for the time I spent on it, you wouldn't be able to afford it." I am sure he was right. There aren't any Terrys around anymore, at least I haven't met any; but I wish there were.

I know for a fact that many times Terry charged me less than he should of for the work he did. I probably wasn't the only one that got a deal either. He was just that way.

The thought of not having a Terry in Texas was a something I didn't really want to think about. It would be hard to start over, and finding a trustworthy mechanic would probably be challenging.

In 2010, I was looking through John Muir's book, *How to keep your Volkswagen Alive (A manual of step by step procedures for the Compleate Idiot)* as part of providing help to a member of the 1966 beetle website. After answering a member's mechanical question, I thought about reaching out to John Muir's widow, Eve, and thanking her for what a profound impact their book had not only on me, but all VW owners.

174

It took a bit of research but I did locate her on Facebook and was able to message her. I really had no expectation of her replying to my message, and that really wasn't the point. I just wanted to thank her.

A day later I received a very nice reply from Eve Muir, that I have included after the forward of this book. It has been a message that I save to this day.

Time flew by between work, the website, VW shows, and vintage motorcycle restorations. Then four years after buying the property in Texas, I retired. Now it would be a matter of putting our Pleasant Prairie house on the market.

The problem at this point was that the housing market in Wisconsin was absolutely horrible. Some folks in our neighborhood had just walked away from their mortgages due to the crash of 2008. This had created short-sales, and bank repossessions over the past few years. All of that had a very negative impact on the property values. The way things were looking, our house might take years to sell.

We now had two birds, a Pionus parrot and a Cockatiel; plus, three dogs. Any time we wanted to show the house, it was an absolute circus. We had to get all the dog stuff put away, cover the bird cages, then load the dogs into my truck and drive around aimlessly as the house was shown.

What became apparent pretty quickly was that most of the people looking at houses during this period, were not serious buyers. They were out just window shopping. I know this is true because of all the photos that accompanied our listing. They showed the house in great detail, and yet potential "buyers" would say "Oh, it has blue carpeting" or "The family room has vaulted ceilings." All of this led to a great deal of frustration on my part, because none of this should have been a surprise to serious buyers.

After about eight home showings, I called the realtors and told them that they needed to do a better job of screening, because I wasn't going through the dog/bird drill anymore for folks that were just trying to find a way to spend their day.

In addition, since I had the Sea Blue bug in the garage, I made it very clear, that buyers could look in the garage but that no one was allowed near the car. This wasn't so much aimed at the adults, but rather kids that might think it was ok to get up close and personal with it.

When fall arrived during the second year of being on the market, I removed the listing. I decided to give us all a break from any more home invasions during the fall and winter months.

It wasn't long after removing the listing that a woman found out from our Neighborhood Association President that our house had been for sale, and she was in the market. The first time she cold called me about our house she made me an offer that was unacceptable, and I said "This house isn't for you, but good luck in your search."

A few weeks later she called back and wanted to see the property ASAP. This happened in the middle of a Green Bay Packer game, which is a big no-no in Wisconsin. That part did not thrill Tammy.

I told her, if you are o.k. with German shepherds, you can come over now, otherwise it will need to be another day. She told me she grew up with shepherds and loved them. Two hours later she made Tammy and I a reasonable offer and we accepted it.

The next day, on December 24th, we broke the news to the kids when they came over for Christmas Eve. My son in law Bob, looked down and said "Worst Christmas ever." I told him, "Look at the bright side, now you have a place to vacation."

The next eight weeks were full of trips to Texas with my cargo trailer, loading our newly built shop with boxes, motorcycles, and the 1966 bug.

When I drove the 66 to Texas, I could hear Terry in the back of my mind throughout the trip saying "Don't push it, it's a small motor, think about how fast those valves are moving when you're going 65 miles an hour."

It ran beautifully all the way to Texas, and I did not "push it", I took it nice an easy all the way.

On February 11th we had the closing on the house in Pleasant Prairie, and headed to Texas. I was going to rent a house not far from the new neighborhood. Tammy would remain in Wisconsin working for a few months and then she stayed on after that to be with Jennifer, as she was now going to have a baby. Her stay extended after the birth of our grandson Trent.

Meanwhile, for me, Texas was a warm paradise compared to Wisconsin. The girls (puppies) and I were out constantly enjoying the weather. When we weren't in the yard, we were overseeing the construction of the house, at the shop sorting out boxes, or getting things ready for the eventual move of everything into the house.

I moved into the new house in May, and Tammy came down in mid-June. It was fantastic to be out of the rental and into our own house.

At this point the shop was now empty, with the exception of the 66, the motorcycles, a bar, and some storage items. Now I could easily move the bug in and out of the shop for drives.

The new home for the Sea Blue Beetle.

Here's where my whole idea of being able to drive a classic beetle all year round in Texas was a little flawed. While it is certainly possible to drive all year round, that is probably only partially true; at least for me. The summer months in Texas are often times brutal. I don't feel comfortable making an air-cooled engine run in those conditions. Just like I didn't like running it while it was hot during the parade in Kenosha.

Now while July, August, and September can be pretty hot, the rest of the year is for the most part great, tornadoes and hail aside.

So, even though I was approaching the hottest time of the year, I began asking if there were any decent classic VW repair places in the DFW area. My new friend Steve, who was actually the building superintendent for our builder, told me about a gentleman out at a nearby airport that worked on air cooled beetles.

My curiosity was peaked so I headed out with my Sea Blue beetle to check out Doug and his VW shop.

What I found is that Doug did a lot more than just work on air cooled beetles. Beetles are probably the smallest part of what he does as his main business is supporting aviation fabrication.

Doug gave me a pretty in-depth tour of his shop that related to VWs. He had the cleanest shop I had ever seen, and some pretty sophisticated equipment. It was an impressive set up, and Doug was a very friendly guy.

After the tour, we went outside and Doug checked out my Sea Blue beetle. Then he turned to me and said "You know there is a group of VW owners that meet monthly in Garland. The group is run by a guy named Jay. He's pretty particular about who he lets join the meeting, but if you're interested in something like that, I can pass your name and phone number along. Of course, I said yes.

A couple days later I received a call from Jay, inviting me to come to Garland and meet for breakfast. So maybe now, I would finally be in a group that would meet regularly.

We met a few days later and had a great talk. I told him about my website for 66 owners, and my history with the VW's I had owned. Jay has a passion for the '67 model in the same way I feel about the '66. I would also put him in the "Purist" category, although he is probably less "judgy" than I am about that kind of thing.

At the end of our meeting Jay invited me to come to "The Gathering" which is what he had named the VW meeting when it started.

Jay stated years later in an email to all of us: "Do NOT think that you are off the hook if you haven't been coming to meetings…Not at all. We still look for everyone to come (when you can, of course). The input from Members is what drives our group. We don't have elections; we don't take membership dues; we don't do charity runs, etc.; We just meet, enjoy one another's VWs and one another. AND—we, together, have Solved SO MANY VW PROBLEMS!" He was right, it was about more than just the beetles.

A Saturday at "The Gathering" in Garland Texas.

You would look high and low to find a nicer group of people than the ones that Jay has put together. I would say most of the members have mechanical skill sets well above mine, and have rebuilt their own engines. If I had an issue, there would be no lack of help coming from this group, and that would be the case a couple years later when a weird series of events caused a major failure on my Sea Blue beetle.

Chapter 17 – Oh God… Now I'm one of those People!"

It's November of 2018 and I began to notice while I am driving to the VW meeting, that the beetle, just doesn't feel quite right. The beetle acts as if the tires are low on air. At intersections, I usually roll back or forward quite easily as I wait for the light to change. This wasn't the case on that particular day. However, I check the tire inflation regularly, so I start to think, perhaps it is all in my mind.

After the meeting I was driving home, and I felt a drop on the left front end of the beetle. "Great a flat" I think. However, then out of the corner of my eye, I see something flying by the side of the car. It is my driver's side front tire. Immediately I think "Oh God, now I am one of those people!"

Who are those people you may ask? Well, they are the ones that do not maintain their cars. They don't check the air pressure, brake fluid, lug nuts, or tire tread.

I once stopped to help a woman stranded on the side of a major road in Wisconsin, not long before we moved. When I drove by, she was on the back side of her car looking at a flat tire. She was wearing "scrubs" so I assumed she might be coming from or going to a medical facility. I immediately did a U-turn and pulled up behind her car.

Although she told me that her husband was on the way, she mentioned that he was riding his bicycle there. I told her I would change her tire. I jacked the car up, and removed the lug nuts. Then as I place a hand on each side of the tire to pull the tire off, I was punctured by sharp shards of the steel belts. It actually punctured the skin on my left hand.

I put the tire to the side and I told the woman "You can't drive on tires like this, it's dangerous" and she said "I know, I need new tires."

I went to her trunk and pulled the spare out, which was every bit as bad as the one that just went flat.

After putting that on the car I told her she should drive right to a tire shop. I told her that some tire shops even sell used tires, and even a used set of tires would be better than what she had on that car.

She thanked me and I hopped back in my car and pulled away, just as her husband came pedaling up the shoulder of the road.

Now I was one of those people, apparently!

So, as the tire sails by me, I hear a loud scraping noise as the hub of the wheel drags on the ground. I pull immediately to the far right lane near a major intersection.

Meanwhile, up ahead I watch my tire cruising at about 45 miles per hour, it proceeds through an intersection, crosses the raised median, and sails across the opposite lane of traffic and up an embankment to a railroad track. It was a miracle that no car was impacted by my tire.

I have to say as I got out of the beetle, I was a bit confused on what to do next. I looked at the front fender well of the bug and I did not really observe any damage. I walked to the sidewalk and called AAA. After that I called Jay, who was still at the VW meeting, just to fill him in on what was happening.

A few minutes later a very nice woman and her daughter pulled up behind my car, and she said "I have your tire." I thanked her and placed the tire on the sidewalk. I thought for sure all the lug nuts would be inside the hub cap when I removed it, but there wasn't a single nut there. How could that even be possible?

When AAA arrived, I told the driver that I had a plan. If we could get the car jacked up, I would take one lug nut off each of the other tires and use those on the front tire to get home.

It took a few minutes for the driver to figure out how he could get the bug off the ground, but he managed to do it without inflicting any damage. Then he waited patiently as I went wheel by wheel collecting lug nuts. Ten minutes later I was cruising home.

Now it made sense to me why, on the way to the meeting, it felt like the tires were low on air. That tire was probably not tracking straight.

When I got home, I called Jay back and he said "Don't worry, I will send you some lug nuts in the mail." He also had a theory on why the tire came off and that was related to the powder coated rims.

Jay felt that the powder coating didn't provide enough of a rough surface for the lug nuts to seat properly to the hub. Now, that might be true, but when I checked all the lug nuts on the other three tires, they were as tight as the day I put them on.

So, in my opinion something else was happening here, but what?

I received Jays lug nuts in the mail with in a day or two and installed them. I double checked every wheel again, because now I was paranoid.

In looking under the fender, I could see how the paint had been rubbed off on the underside of the fenders lip. I could probably live with that, but I also had a strange circular spot on the very middle of the beetle's roof that I had noticed the year before. It almost looked like the tip of an eraser had imprinted the paint. However, around the edge of the dimple, I could see a fine crack in the paint. There had to be rust, or an imperfection in the metal prep that caused this to happen. I decided I would have my local body shop guy, Oscar (aka Rusty of Rusty's Bodywerks), take a look at both of these areas.

Before I could get it in to Rusty's shop, I had another VW meeting. This trip would be worse than the first but it would lead to what I think caused the wheel to come off the 66 beetle.

On the way to the meeting, I still experienced the feeling of low air in the tires, which I knew was not possible. I started to think that it had to be either a wheel bearing or a hung-up brake shoe.

When I got to the parking lot where the meeting takes place, I touched every wheel as I walked around the car. When I got to the wheel that had come off the previous month, it was so hot that I almost burned my hand.

Scott, one of the members, said he was almost positive that I had a wheel cylinder issue, and that the brakes were not releasing on that wheel. After a few minutes Scott backed the brake off of the drum.

After we pushed on the brake pedal again, the problem returned. The consensus of the group was that there were two potential problems:

1. A bad brake line that was not letting fluid flow back out of the cylinder or
2. A bad brake cylinder

I decided at this point that I would try to get home after the meeting by going slow and timing each light so that, if possible, I could avoid using the brakes. Amazingly, that actually worked.

Once I returned home, I decided I would try to trouble shoot the issue. I got on the phone with Scott, and together we replicated the frozen brake issue. Then I located the bleeder valve and I tried letting fluid out of the cylinder to see if the shoes would release; they did not. I decided to let the car sit for the rest of the day and see if the brake shoes would retract (to confirm a hose issue vs. a wheel cylinder). The next morning, the wheel was still frozen.

Next, I tore the wheel apart to look at the cylinder. Surprisingly, a few lug nuts were loose. This is the point where Jays theory and my new theory come together. I believe that when the wheel became hot, it allowed the nuts to loosen because the powder coating expanded. Scott seemed to think the same thing was a possibility stating "it seems just too coincidental to have the wheel come off one day, then have the brakes freeze the next time out"

Next, I inspected the brake cylinder; it was frozen. So, then I called Terry back at Burlington Import Auto. He recommended that I buy all new bearings, seals, and a brake cylinder for the front wheel. As always, I relied on Terry to tell me where I should purchase the parts. I decided that while I was doing this job I might as well just do both front wheels.

Digging into the problem.

The job didn't take very long, with the exception of pounding out the old bearing races. That required much force and profanity as well. Then the bug was back on the road, better than ever. I regularly check these lug nuts before meetings now, and have never had a loose one. I believe this validates my theory about the heat generated on the hub leading to the loosening of the lug nuts.

Well, unfortunately the story doesn't quite end here, for two reasons:

1) My friends at the VW meeting take quite a bit of delight asking me if any tires passed me on the way to or from the meeting.
2) I still needed to get the Sea Blue beetle to the body shop.

So, now that my mechanical issues were in the rearview mirror, so to speak, it was time to go see Rusty about the roof of the beetle.

I think Rusty does the best body work around. I drove to his shop and told him about the wheel episode and wondered if he could just touch up the underside of the fender lip. He walked outside to take a close look at it and said "You actually have more going on here than that, see the small cracks in the paint coming around the lip to the outside of the fender?"

He was absolutely right, that would need to be taken care of. Then I showed him the roof, and the weird spot. He agreed that something underneath probably wasn't prepped correctly prior to its paint job many years back.

Then the big question, would he be able to match the paint? The original paint that VW used in 1966 was a lacquer. The paint used by

Perfection auto body, when I had it repainted in Burlington, was also the same as the original, lacquer. Unfortunately, that lacquer paint had been banned from sale around 2012.

Rusty told me he was sure that he would be able to match the paint, so I was relieved. A week or so later the Sea Blue bug was getting more Sea Blue paint.

The work turned out great, and the beetle once again looked fantastic. It's quite a show piece, and people like checking it out when they come over to the have a beer at the bar.

Of course, nothing lasts forever, and now she drips a little oil from the rear seal.

I have also tracked down a small brake fluid leak with Scotts' help. I have removed the old master cylinder, and replaced it with a new one. It is conveniently (insert sarcasm here) located behind the drivers' side wheel in a place where a contortionist would have issues getting to it. So, getting the new master cylinder hooked up to the old brake lines proved challenging.

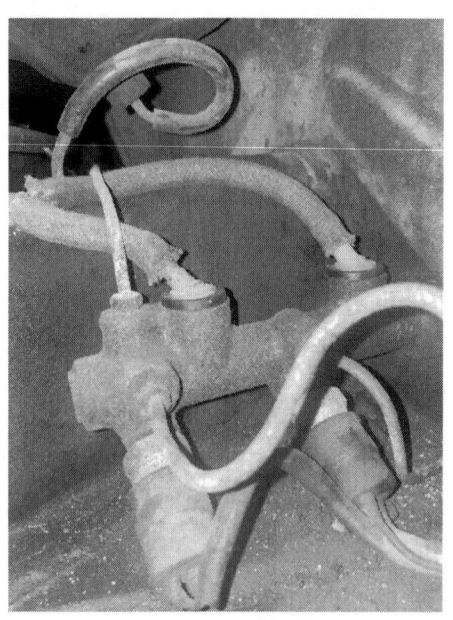

Out with the old!

Scott drilled some holes for the new two compartment brake fluid reservoir. This will give me an additional safety factor, so that if a leak happens at the rear brakes, I would still have front brakes and vice versa. The new reservoir fits nicely, and now all we have left to do is bleed the brake system.

Despite these small issues, for a vehicle that is approaching almost sixty years old, it is a wonderful car.

I have also had this beetle longer than any other vehicle I have owned.

In with the new!

Of course, with any vintage vehicle there are always things that are going to need to be repaired. Some of the problems may be hard to track down.

Over the last few years, I have had an issue where the 66 won't start. I am always able to get it going but it acts as if there is a dead spot on the starter. However, it could be the ignition switch as well. After all it has been used for over 57 years.

Electrical problems are always a source of frustration. In this case I decided to start with the ignition switch and replace it. We are a few months down the road now and I haven't had a single problem. If the problem re-occurs, I will be shopping for a new six-volt starter.

When I replaced the ignition, I had it rekeyed to be the same as the doors, so I don't need to mess around with more than one key.

The engine deck lid also had a lock, but it was an SV key code. My other locks are SC keys, so I had to track down an SC cylinder so I could get that lock rekeyed. As it turned out I could only find one and it was located in Poland. While I don't really plan on locking the engine compartment, I just wanted everything matched to one key. I am just that way.

Chapter 18 – It's always something.

Most VW Beetle owners will say "It's always something". They don't say it to be funny, they say it because it's true.

No matter what classic beetle you have – there's always something that pops up! It could be a mechanical issue or you just might notice that something is missing. Sometimes it's the things you don't ever think to look for that cause you to start a new project. That just happened to be the case with my beetle.

I became involved in an email conversation with Dario, a long-time member of the 1966vwbeetle forum. He had some questions about the metal rail that runs around the back of the rear seat. That got me looking more closely at my bugs interior. Then I started asking some questions of my own.

Way back in 1975 (when I had my first beetle), I was sure that my '66 had a couple of accessories that were now missing from the Sea Blue bug. For those of you that happen to be 1966 beetle owners, turn to page 11 of your owner's manual (if you are lucky enough to have one). You will notice a rear seat retaining strap. This strap is designed to hold the back seat down so that you can put more luggage into the rear of the car. There was no sign of it in my Sea Blue bug.

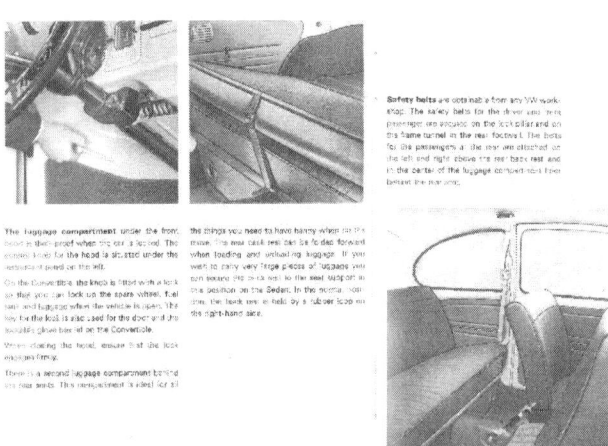

Page 11

You will also see a rubber tie back strap attached to the rear seat near the passenger side wall (just under the ash tray in the middle picture above). That strap is screwed into the back seat frame rail. Then it is stretched backwards and attaches to a metal hook that is screwed into the sidewall. This is designed to hold the rear seat in place, in the event of a collision. That strap is missing on my bug, but the hook is there…and it's broken.

Since I had neither of those straps, that really bothered me. However, they are available to purchase through different aftermarket suppliers.

But wait, there's more! Now, I also discovered something even more disturbing. The rear carpet extending from the lower back of the rear seat into the parcel tray was not attached to the metal channel that holds it in place. A less particular individual might say "who cares", but I wanted it fastened correctly.

In the almost two decades that I've owned the bug, I had never noticed that the carpet wasn't tucked into this channel. I spend absolutely no time behind the back seat, except to store a VW duffel bag. When I need the bag, I just reach over and grab it.

What made this even more perplexing is that no one had a good answer for how that material needed to be pushed into that channel. The most reasonable answer was that a metal bar should have been inside a sleeve of material sewn at the edge of the carpet. Then that end would get hammered into the channel. However, there was no metal bar present inside my carpet sleeve.

It's somewhat interesting to note that the newer carpet kits for the 1966 have a plastic clip sewn into them that slides into that channel. That would make fastening the carpet quick and painless. As luck would have it, I was stuck with the metal bar solution.

It was a shock that my carpet wasn't reattached when it was completed back in 2005. My guess is that the metal bar was missing even then, so the installer just bypassed this step. I have absolutely no idea what happened to the rear seat retaining (luggage) strap, but it had probably rotted away years before, as almost all of them have.

It's sometimes the finer details that get overlooked. Now, it was a matter of getting all of this back to original condition.

Well, there were a few things that I needed to take care of first.

1) A flat stock piece of metal 1/8" x 3/4" x 36" long, needed to be purchased. Dario gave me great measurements on the piece I needed. I found a flat stock piece at Home Depot, but it was 48" long. I cut the flat stock to size when I got home, and then rounded the corners.

2) I found the original 1960's rear seat retaining strap on eBay, and ordered it. It was not in great shape, so I knew I would need to clean it up. I found the rubber hold back strap and metal clip at Wolfsburg West and purchased those as well.

3) The rear seat and rear seat section of carpet needed to be removed. This is where my nightmare began. Obviously, the back seat came out easily since it is just two bolts that hold it in place. Then I took the lower metal piece off of the bottom of the rear seat backrest. This holds the two pieces of carpet together. Once I removed that the carpet on the back seat, it puckered so I added 3M Adhesive to my shopping list. The only reason I removed this is that somewhere in my twisted brain I thought I could attach the rear piece in the channel and then flip it over and attach it to the seat back. That is an impossibility, the section MUST be attached to the seat back first.

Now the seat went back in and the hellish hammering began to no avail. Then after working on the carpet for thirty minutes with no success, I went in the house to take a shower.

A little later on I began spreading the channels track gently with a crowbar to allow for an easier fit. Even though the bar itself would easily fit inside the track, once the carpeting was added, it was too tight of a fit. So, after multiple attempts to get it in the channel I thought, "This work would be more easily done by someone who has the right tools to spread that track wider, without damaging it".

I made a quick visit back to Rusty's Bodywerks and in a few quick minutes, they found a way to easily spread the channel and insert the carpet.

Carpeting now attached!

One would think that this would be the end to a perfect day, and it almost was, until a truck going the opposite way on the highway threw a rock at my front fender and damaged it. So, I ended up back at Rusty's the following week for that repair as well. It's always something!

While the bug was at Rusty's Bodywerks, I started working on the used retaining strap. I polished the old buckle, and dyed the strap back to a grey color. All the original straps were grey but over time bleached out into a kind of yellow/khaki color.

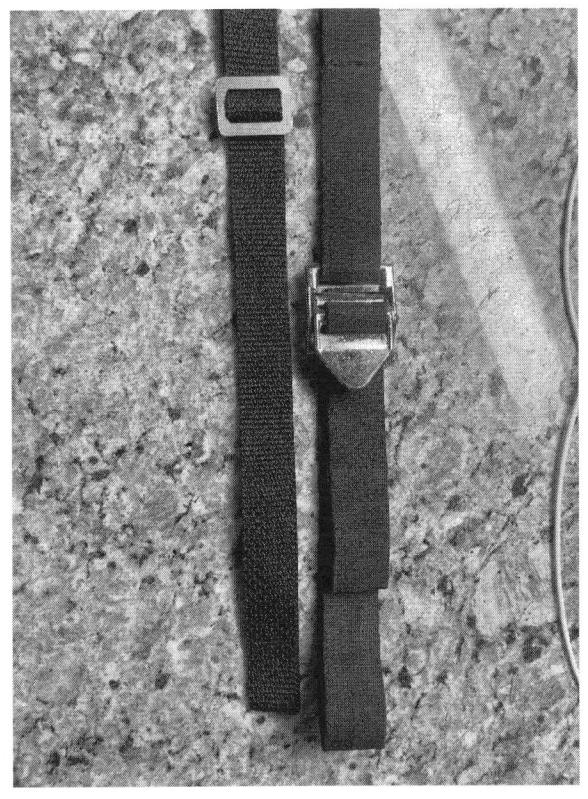

The finished strap.

Dying the strap was not fun. It's a multistep process. Suffice it to say that it was a lot of tedious work that took more than a couple of hours. However, the end result was very nice.

Once I started to install it, I realized the original strap was not quite long enough. This is probably due to the way it had been removed from the original car. However, I did get it to fit – just barely. I'm hoping that over time that it will stretch.

In the above picture you can see the strap inserted in the top rail, and the lower clip inside the lower back seat cushion support rail (just like page 11 of the owner's manual!). In addition, if you look really close you can see the rubber seat strap that holds the seat back in place, when it is used as a passenger seat. That strap is next to the passenger side wall and hooks into the metal clip, which you can see above the rear speaker.

So, what did I learn from this rear seat fiasco??

1) It's great to have purist friends like Dario to send a multitude of pictures to help source and install the strap. The folks in my VW group, were also helpful, and curious about how all of this would fit together. In fact, some didn't know anything about the strap, since few cars still have them.

2) You can find aftermarket straps that will work. They will get the job done if you are just looking for something functional but not authentic. I can understand using one of the aftermarket straps, since you won't be required to futz around as much as I did.

3) There is not a lot of space for the lower clip as it fits into the lower track under the rear seat cushion. It's best to insert the curved part first then pull it upwards. I was hoping I could gain a little more space between the rear seat cushion and the rail but that was a pipe dream.

4) Any vintage strap that you buy is probably going to be faded. You may choose to dye

it back to a grey color, and that will be fun – not really.

5) There is a definite lack of information available regarding the strap, so it can be frustrating. In addition, you will probably find that when you search on "Retaining Strap", you end up with the little rubber seat strap that attaches to the metal hook. This too, tends to be frustrating.

6) You won't find the metal anchor band that originally fastened the strap to the rear seat under the carpet. Ask me how I know. Hours of looking and I found nothing about it. To me, that is not a big deal because any flat piece of metal with a few screws would work. However, you would need a large enough strap to reach that area, and I do not. Plus, I don't want to remove my carpet. This again speaks to how VW missed the boat on continuing to support the VW culture with original parts.

7) The on-line community, such as thesamba.com, Chris Vallone from Classic VW Bugs, and the vintage Volkswagen groups on Facebook become a great

resource when searching for information about old parts.

8) The retaining strap was a smart design from VW, just not explained well or really featured much in their owner's manual.

In conclusion, (if there really is one), you will never run out of things to work on when it comes to a classic beetle. It may be simple maintenance, a repair, or it may be something cosmetic. No matter what the case, you will have some sort of an adventure. It could be mundane, fun, or completely frustrating, but in the end, hopefully you end up in a happy place!

Chapter 19 –Epilogue

I still stay in touch with Dennis, and we have a lot of history together. When I talk to Dennis it is as if time has stood still over all these years. He is one of a handful of folks that I have that type of relationship with.

I have known Dennis since I was 16, it is the longest friendship I have maintained. Dennis and I share experiences together going back fifty years; starting as friends, then working together, and then going to college in Madison at the same time.

Most of our history borders on the hilarious, primarily due to Dennis and his "shock humor". It's not for everyone, but it definitely has always worked for me.

I'm looking forward to a time when he can visit here in Texas, and we can take the 66 for a nice long cruise.

In 2010 I tried to find out what happened to "Toms Barn". I was able to contact a previous employee named Charles. Charles told me that the area where the barn was located is now completely developed into housing. He always assumed the urban sprawl is what spelled the demise to "The Barn". He had no idea what happened to Tom after he quit working there. He said Tom was always taking off to do trading in futures markets, and perhaps he had made it big at some point!

I still call Terry on occasion to get his advice. He is always helpful, and he probably has enough stories that he could write his own book. I'll share one quick story because it is pretty entertaining.

Terry had a customer that kept coming into his shop complaining of a brake fluid leak. Terry would look at the car and say he "couldn't find any leak". Of course, the customer was frustrated because he was certain of it since he had seen brake fluid on the wheel rim.

After a few visits with no success finding any leak, the gentleman returned. He told Terry he had the proof of the leak because the fluid was still on the rim of the car.

Terry went outside and looked at the rim, bent down, and then ran his finger in the fluid and then smelled it. He knew exactly what the problem was.

He returned to the waiting area of his shop and told the customer "You don't have a brake fluid leak; you have a dog that is urinating on your tire".

Terry has a lot of stories like that, because he has been dealing with VW customers for almost his entire life.

Now that he is retired, he has moved away from working on VW's, even as a hobby, at least for now. I told him once that I'd love to flat bed my 66 to Wisconsin and have him do the main oil seal. His response was "I don't do that anymore".

As I have issues with my beetle, and I do, I will reach out to Terry for advice. The last time I talked to him it was about the ignition system. He is an encyclopedia of VW knowledge. Prior to that conversation we talked about getting new tires for the beetle.

He has a mind like a steel trap and talked about the original tire size, which was 5.16 x 15. That is the size of my spare tire, an old firestone, but the rest of my tires are 165/80/R15. Terry warned me to be very careful with that size tire in the trunk and "Make sure it fits before they slam the hood down on it, and bend your hood." Then he said "Once you talk to them for a while, they'll know they need to be careful with your bug."

I would love to replace the rear engine seal at some point and I know there are folks that would be willing to help from the VW club. I just need to decide when to pull the trigger on that repair. It's not that it needs to be done, it just bothers me.

While the 6-volt system is not great, I don't plan on changing to 12-volts. I would love to have the brighter lights but I don't want to change how it came from the factory. I rarely drive at night so it really is a non- issue for me.

When the beetle is not in use, I am surrounded in my office by classic beetle books, advertisements most from 1966, the Sea Blue's birth certificate from Wolfsburg, Germany, and some of the awards that the Sea Blue took at shows in Wisconsin, and now in Texas. So, I am never far away from the VW culture.

I know at some point, hopefully way in the distant future, my Sea Blue Beetle will be with someone else. Hopefully it will be with someone who also has a 1966 Beetle Obsession. Until then, she will sit safely in her spot waiting for the next ride.

The adventure continues…

Printed in Great Britain
by Amazon

53814795R00121